winter
stars

an elderly mother, an aging son,
and life's final jouney

winter stars

*an elderly mother, an aging son,
and life's final jouney*

Dave Iverson

Durham, NC

Published 2022, by Light Messages Publishing
www.lightmessages.com
Durham, NC 27713 USA
SAN: 920-9298

Paperback ISBN: 978-1-61153-448-1
Hardcover ISBN: 978-1-61153-463-4
E-book ISBN: 978-1-61153-449-8
Library of Congress Control Number: 2021950535

All royalties from the sale of *Winter Stars* go to support:
The Michael J. Fox Foundation for Parkinson's Research;
Dance for PD; and Avenidas, a San Francisco Bay Area
organization providing caregiver support.

For Adelaide
Eileen and Sinai
and Lynn

PROLOGUE

IN THE FALL OF 2013, I walked into the kitchen of my mom's house in Menlo Park, California. She was 101 years old, and the early stages of dementia were beginning to take hold. She looked up at me and said:

> I think there are two Adelaides.
> There's the good Adelaide—
> the one who's pretty and smart
> and knows how to do things.
> And there's the bad Adelaide—
> the one who's ugly and stupid
> and can't do anything.
>
> I'm not sure which one is here right
> now, but I think it's the bad Adelaide.

✦

My mom had always been a force. She'd graduated from high school at age sixteen, from college at twenty— and at the top of her class in both. She'd been a teacher, a devoted spouse, a mother of three, a passionate sports fan, a loyal friend, and a powerhouse volunteer. When she was ninety-four, she threw out the first pitch at a Stanford University baseball game. At ninety-six, she made phone calls, in her own distinctive style, urging people to vote for Barack Obama.

Now the long arc of her remarkable life was turning in a new direction, yet she'd been able to describe what was happening to her with searing precision—and without tears. She was like that. She didn't blink, confronting most challenges with a firm, no-nonsense demeanor. No one ever trifled with Adelaide Iverson, and that included me.

I'd moved in with my mom six years before. After my dad died, she'd lived independently for thirteen years. But at age ninety-five, she had a difficult bout with pneumonia and couldn't manage fully on her own. I was a broadcaster and filmmaker, living in nearby San Francisco at the time. My life was full but flexible, and it didn't take much deliberation to decide that it just made sense for me to move in and help. My mom and I had always been close. We shared interests and passions. But more than that, there'd always been a certain ease to our relationship. We understood each other. We were a comfortable pairing. And with that, at the age of fifty-nine, I moved back into my boyhood home.

But there was a great deal I didn't know. I didn't know I would become so exhausted. I didn't know I would be capable of getting so angry. I didn't know that I would be tested in ways I'd never imagined, or rewarded in ways I'd never dreamed. I didn't know that someone with dementia can still be poetic, or that I'd get proficient at transferring my mom from bed to commode and back again, but never quite master the intimate skill of changing diapers. I didn't know I'd be joined and strengthened by remarkable women caregivers who became my teachers, my comrades, and my kin. Or that I'd discover that the Parkinson's disease I'd been diagnosed with a few years before would present fewer challenges than being a caregiver. I didn't anticipate that during this time, the two most meaningful professional experiences of my life would take place, or that I'd wind up getting married. And I never imagined that after I moved back in, my mom would live for another full decade, before passing away at the age of 105.

The ten-year caregiving odyssey we shared affected me, humbled me, and reoriented me more than any other experience in my life. And during that decade together, my mom and I drew closer—I'd like to think, both to each other and to our truest selves.

This is the story of our journey, and of the remarkable women who accompanied us and changed our lives.

I

SETTING FORTH

1

THE TEN-SECOND DECISION

EVERYONE THOUGHT MY PARENTS had a terrific marriage, because they did. My dad had a wonderful career as a professor and dean at Stanford University, but everyone knew it was my mom who was the real force to reckon with. My dad knew it, too, and he loved her for it.

World War II may have delayed the start of their life together, but that long separation also fueled their romance and forged their lasting bond. My parents adored each other. They were Adelaide and Bill. Always. Nothing could change that, including my dad's final years with Parkinson's disease, which they managed as they'd managed everything. Together.

My parents had been married just over fifty years when my dad passed away in 1994, at the age of eighty-two. We had a lovely memorial, attended by hundreds of friends and family.

At the close of an emotional service, my mom remained sitting for a few moments, and then she stood up smartly and said, "Well, let's get going."

She'd loved my dad with ferocious loyalty, but she was never one for lingering goodbyes. She always focused on what she was going to do next.

For the next thirteen years, my Mom led a determined life, living alone in the Menlo Park home where my brothers and I had grown up. For more than half of that time, she continued to drive—and she drove well. She visited friends and family, attended Stanford University sports events, League of Women Voters meetings, movies, and the theater. Once, she told me how she still missed putting her arm around my dad at night. But she didn't pine for their shared past, even while continuing to cherish the life she'd had with him.

And she was that way about her own life story, too. She remembered everything: what she wore to a ball at the University of Michigan, what score she got on a particular test, where anyone and everyone went to college. She had an interior card catalogue for all of it, but the past didn't orient her daily priorities. It was the same with old grievances. She was fully capable of holding onto grudges, but she didn't nurse or cultivate them. She just filed them away on the shelves of her prodigious memory, and only brought them out for display when she felt it was useful to do so.

She carried her life story with her, but she didn't want to live there. I think that's why she read *The New York Times* cover to cover every morning until she was past a hundred years old. She was attached to the present, and as important, to action more than interior reflection. She was a very smart person, but hers was more a life in motion than a life of the mind.

And as I think about what contributed to her vibrant old age, perhaps no quality mattered more than her lack of apprehension. She didn't long for what was, nor did she fret about the future. Even after the death of my dad—the man she had loved and built her life around—she knew she'd be OK.

So in 2002, on her ninetieth birthday, she did something I'd never heard of anyone her age doing. She cut up her driver's license. Until that moment, she'd always driven to see her pals on the Stanford campus, or to San Francisco, or down the California coast to Carmel. As is true for so many late in life, driving had seemed central to her ability to maintain a sense of independence. But she said getting rid of her license was an easy decision.

"It's just time," she said. "I want to quit while I'm ahead."

And she had a plan for how she'd continue to maintain her active life. She'd budgeted $200 a month for cabs to get around town, and figured she could still take the train to San Francisco.

Her plan worked well, save the time she got her scarf caught in a newspaper vending machine at the Menlo Park train station, and couldn't extricate herself until a harried commuter plunked in an extra quarter so that she could be on her way—newspaper in hand, of course.

Her life was not going to change, just the means to lead it. From reading to friends who no longer could, to getting her hair done each week, she wasn't about to curtail her activities. I would play a minor supporting role. I'd moved back to the Bay Area in 2001, after spending most of my professional life in the Midwest, and would come down from San Francisco for weekend visits. Now, those visits simply included additional trips to the grocery store, and more crucially, to Stanford sports events.

My mom had loved sports since she'd moved to Lawrence, Kansas as a little girl. Her father had taken her to Kansas University games, and she'd gone to grade school with the son of James Naismith, the man who invented basketball. To this day, our extended family conducts the annual James Naismith–Adelaide Iverson NCAA Basketball Brackets Competition. Not surprisingly, she won more often than any of us.

But baseball was her favorite sport, and she loved going to Sunken Diamond, home to the Stanford baseball team, and one of the prettiest little ballparks in America. She'd taken my brothers and me to games there when we were little, and we'd run around throughout the game, chasing the foul balls that sailed into the stands. And now it was my turn to take her.

Few things made my mom happier than walking into the ballpark and looking out at the green grass, with the campus and the Stanford foothills framed over the right-field wall. Old friends would come over to greet her. She was easy to spot; her carefully coiffed, snow-white hair and cardinal-red Stanford baseball cap stood out in the stands.

One sunny afternoon, when we were sitting at a ball game together, I began to do one of those mental exercises that only a sport with baseball's particular rhythm allows. I started trying to figure out how many Stanford games my mom had been to since my folks arrived on campus in the mid-1940s. As the game unfolded, I estimated that between 1946 and 1991, when my dad stopped being able to attend, my parents had gone to well over a thousand football, basketball, and baseball games. And in the fifteen years since that time, my mom had attended at least several hundred more, bringing her total attendance at Stanford sporting events to something like thirteen hundred games over a sixty-year span. This deserved some sort of celebration.

And so in 2006, I arranged to have my mom throw out the first pitch at a Stanford game. She was about to turn ninety-four, and she was psyched. We planned a big party at the ballpark. Friends and relatives came from all over. My daughter flew in from Boston and practiced playing catch with her in the days leading up to the big event. And when it was time to walk her out to the mound, she put on her best game face, tugged at the bill of her Stanford baseball cap, and headed out onto the sunlit field.

After her ten-foot toss to a Stanford player, the team came out to greet her. She high-fived everyone as the crowd applauded. The players responded with equal enthusiasm, and as we approached the end of the line, one of the coaches said, "You know, we could use another reliever this season, and it looks like you've got a pretty good arm."

✦

And on she went. Besides going to games and the theater, she filled her hours with friends, good books, *The Times*, the latest films, and long walks. In the evening, she poured herself a stiff scotch, watched the *PBS NewsHour*, then searched the TV listings for a ball game. I don't think it ever occurred to her that she wouldn't always be able to go on like this. And her indomitable spirit allowed the rest of us to avoid thinking about what the future might hold for her as well.

It wasn't until 2007, when she'd reached the age of ninety-five, that Adelaide's world would tilt in a new direction. She got pneumonia. The early warning signs were there—a persistent cough and wheeze—but my mom was tough, and like most women I know, far more stoic than men when it came to dealing with physical maladies. She wasn't sick, she said, and refused to go to the doctor. But a week later, I noticed she also seemed slightly confused, and Adelaide Iverson was never, ever confused.

To her great unhappiness, I made her go with me to the clinic. Once there, her doctor ordered an X-ray. And then in short order, a sequence of events took place that, looking back, marked a turning point in both our lives. We were led to a prep room, and after the nurse closed the door, I realized it was up to me to help my mom undress and put on a hospital gown. She wasn't embarrassed, just deeply annoyed that all this was happening to her. Nor was she undone when we received the doctor's pneumonia diagnosis a short time later. She just wanted to assign responsibility.

She looked at me with a fearsome expression and said, "You have betrayed me."

And then, for the first time, I pushed her out to the car, in a wheelchair.

The usual antibiotics didn't do the trick. She grew worse and had to be hospitalized. She had a rough time, and as those long hospital nights unfolded, it began to sink in that everything was about to change. She was not going to be able to manage on her own any longer.

Thanks to wonderful care and an extended hospital stay, she did get marginally stronger physically, but impressively stronger mentally. It would soon be time to head home.

As the day of her hospital discharge approached, I decided, with no small amount of trepidation, that I needed to talk to her about getting help at home. She didn't blink, readily agreeing to my suggestion. I shouldn't have been surprised. It was just another example of her ability to adjust to life's setbacks, and she was nothing if not practical. What mattered was maintaining her way of life, and if that involved a few necessary props, then so be it.

She chose to act as if these new supports were the most natural thing in the world. Have someone come in and help cook? Why not? Use a walker from now on? Of course. Just as she'd chosen to stop driving, she now chose to have a supporting cast.

I contacted a home care agency a friend had recommended, and my mom and I interviewed several prospective candidates while she was still at the hospital. We were both drawn to a woman named Tila Langhi, and she was parked in our driveway when I drove my mom home.

I walked Tila around the house and showed her where to find things. When we were done, she had just one question: "Where do you keep gloves?"

I stared at her with a blank expression. "Gloves?"

She smiled. "You know, the gloves I'll need to wear when I help your mom in the bathroom."

In time, I would become expert in the art of getting gloves on quickly enough to assist with the task that would follow. But at that moment, I just said, "Right. Gloves. I'll go get some."

Tila was great, a certified nursing assistant who possessed the competence and caring that we needed, but she could only be there six hours a day. I knew almost instantly that my mom needed more help, both at night and on the weekend, and it took me all of ten seconds to decide that the extra helper would be me. I was a self-employed documentary filmmaker, and part-time NPR radio host in San Francisco, and I had plenty of work flexibility. Plus, I was single. My longtime companion, Lynn, was unfailingly understanding, and my recently married daughter was living an active life on the East Coast. My two brothers were both dealing with health issues of their own, and one of them lived out of state. My work was just thirty miles away, and my mom and I had always enjoyed each other. And even though I'd been diagnosed with Parkinson's a few years before, so far I was doing extremely well. Besides, given my mom's age, it wasn't like this would be a permanent arrangement. It all seemed pretty straightforward.

And with that, at the age of fifty-nine, I moved in with my mom.

2

SETTING FORTH

IT WASN'T LONG BEFORE I LEARNED something fundamental: paid caregivers have lives of their own. On
occasion, I'd get an early morning call from the agency,
informing me that Tila was ill, or that she had to stay
home because one of her kids was sick. Somehow, I had
never anticipated this. I thought I had everything figured
out, and that despite living with my mom, the rest of my
life would return to normal.

It didn't. And it never would. But I didn't know that
yet.

It hadn't occurred to me that problems would not
only arise, but that I'd be the only person available to
solve them. Each one unanticipated. Each one with
consequences that could turn your day or week upside
down, because whatever else was on your to-do list, it no
longer mattered.

Home care agencies offer replacement helpers, but as
I began to discover, those arrangements always involve

delays, and are often deficient, through no particular fault of anyone. For starters, they won't know where the gloves are. Nor were they likely to be an equal match for my mom. The agency replacement helpers would either be intimidated by her, or she would be critical of their efforts—often both. So I made what seemed like another obvious decision, given the flexible nature of my work. I wouldn't just be there at night and on the weekend. I'd be first in line for backup as well. It would just be so much simpler.

Caregiving doesn't offer decision points at convenient intervals, and without having thought about it, I'd established a new normal—and norms are never easy to change. My mom assumed I would always be there, not only on nights and weekends, but whenever needed. Anyone in her position would do the same. The more significant presumption was mine: *Of course* I can do this.

Caregiving has a way of accentuating your character traits for good or ill, and one of mine was the need to take charge—a touch of hubris that would lead to plenty of unintended life-with-Mom consequences in the years ahead.

Still, early on, we mostly managed. I was more cabbie and cook than anything else. Our easy rapport, bolstered by a common passion for sports and politics, served us well. Before I'd moved in, taking my mom to occasional baseball games had been a pleasant pastime. But now I was learning that there was nothing like attending a football game with someone approaching a hundred, who yells, "Tackle 'em'! Get that guy! Get 'em!"

I took pride in relaying stories like that to friends and

family, and would modestly demur when they told me what a fine thing I was doing.

To be sure there were times when I'd shake my head and wonder what in the world I was doing. I'd retreat to my childhood bedroom at night and look around at a space that had not changed in the past fifty years. It was still painted beige. The same brown and white carpet still covered the floor. The artwork that hung on the wall was unchanged, too, including a print of the Dutch countryside from our family trip to Europe in 1962. My old high school speech and drama awards still occupied one corner of my childhood desk. And the bookshelf was filled with mostly the same books, though one notable volume was missing—one my dad had given me when I was twelve.

I could still remember how he'd walked in one evening and placed a thin book with a dark-blue cover on the shelf. As he turned to go, he said, "You might want to look at that sometime," and then slipped out the door. I'd picked it up that evening and started reading, astonished by what I was taking in: a prim and proper explanation, with as little anatomical detail as possible, of the facts of life.

And now, nearly fifty years later, I was back in that same bedroom. Even the twin beds were still there— mine covered by the same striped bedspread, with a red Stanford blanket underneath. Sometimes I'd wake up in the middle of the night and think, "I'm almost sixty years old, and I'm sleeping in the same single bed I had when I was twelve. *This is pretty damn weird.*"

But the truth is, those first few months weren't that

hard. We got by, which I would learn counts as an A-rating in caregiving. Except when Tila's children got sick, I mostly had enough help. I could still do the work that mattered to me. And when Tila left in the late afternoon, I took over and managed nights and weekends the best I could—sharing meals, sports, and the latest news. Nearby friends and family would visit. And just as crucial, my partner, Lynn, would come down from Berkeley one night a week. Her presence provided support and a semblance of normality—and it finally inspired me to get a new bed.

It was all going to be OK.

And then, just six months into her time with us, Tila told me she was pregnant and wouldn't be able to continue working with Adelaide and me.

✦

The question I probably asked the most during my time as a caregiver was, "Now what?" Whenever I thought I'd figured things out, I hadn't. My solutions usually worked—until they didn't. In fact, about the only aspect of caregiving that stays the same is the ongoing task of finding the right person to help—a challenge I would confront, then solve, then confront again.

After Tila left, a good friend recommended a caregiver who'd previously helped take care of her mother. Getting a reference isn't always critical in hiring situations, but getting a caregiver recommendation from a trusted friend is gold. Like Tila, Mele Taufa was a woman of Tongan descent, and part of the broad Pacific Islander community who form the backbone of the caregiving community in the Bay Area. Mele, twenty years old and newly married, possessed a warm smile and easy laugh. She had an unrelentingly joyful approach to life. And while joyful probably isn't the first attribute you'd think to put on your list of desirable caregiver qualities, having someone who adds unsinkable cheerfulness to your household is no small thing. Mele brought a great, good-natured presence into any room, and there are few things a supportive caregiver can offer that are more helpful than that.

You can approach hiring a caregiver in many different ways. But I came to think about it like this: How am I going to feel about a prospective caregiver showing up when my day—not to mention, my mom's—depends on her? Do I feel relieved when this person arrives at the front door, or am I anxious about what will happen next?

I knew after meeting Mele that her daily arrival would make me smile—my mom, too. And that's probably one of the best indicators of whether a potential caregiver is going to work out.

+

Sometimes I still think about all the consequences that stemmed from my ten-second decision to move in with my mom. And yet, when people ask me today if I would do it again, my answer is yes.

That doesn't mean I'd do it the same way; assuming any aspect of the caregiving experience is definitive is a fool's errand. What you think of as defining moments turn out not to be, and because things keep changing, today's challenges will eventually become the good old days. But that very upending is also what makes the experience revealing and life altering. You are tried in ways you can't imagine. You fail in ways you'd never dreamed. And if you're as lucky as I was, you'll be challenged and enriched to your very soul.

✦

It begins with the elemental nature of what must be done—to feed, care for, clean, and clothe another human being. And as adults, we are almost always completely unprepared to do that. Yes, if you're a parent, you once did this for your child. And yes, there can be striking similarities between what you need to do for a young child, and what you need to do for an aging parent. But if you've tried changing diapers for both, you already know how very different the tasks feel.

We anticipate and long for the opportunity to care for a child. But unlike the anticipation, preparation, and excitement that comes with the arrival of a newborn, we often plunge into caring for a parent without planning or forethought. Somehow, we manage not to anticipate this eventuality. Or when we do, we manage to dismiss it from our consciousness as soon as possible. We move on to more pressing topics, like what to make for dinner.

Deciding to have a child usually features excited conversations with spouses or partners and friends about what might lie ahead. We buy books, attend classes, and browse an infinite number of parenting websites. But the reality of caring for a parent lands on your doorstep with less joy than the proverbial stork. And while it's true that no one is fully prepared to become a parent, I think only a minute few are prepared to *care for* a parent. There isn't the caregiving equivalent of a child development chart that marks when first words are formed, or second naps come to an end. Instead, you discover that the next stage of caregiving isn't self-evident or predictable, or even a next stage at all.

And so we set out on one of life's most challenging journeys, like one of those early explorers bound for terra incognita. You leave without a good map, and you don't know where you're going or how long the journey will last. Rough patches are followed by smooth, and then you're surprised all over again when the next storm emerges. You find that no matter what you've learned, it does not predict what lies ahead. And you learn that once you're onboard as a caregiver, it's hard to turn around and go back, harder still to disembark.

In the end, you find that it's difficult to even know what the goal of this journey really is. Is it to extend life? Or merely to extend quality of life? And by the way, what does that ubiquitous phrase actually mean?

Until she was ninety-five, my mom was someone who would no more have wanted to spend the last years of her life bedridden, than vote Republican. But as time went on, she clung to life with the same ferocity that governed her other loyalties.

The truth is, the purpose, meaning, and even the hoped-for destination of this journey becomes *less* clear over time. Horizons shift. Landfall becomes more shrouded. And even when you sense you may finally be approaching the journey's end, you find that you do so with both dread and yearning.

We begin this odyssey not knowing how little we know. At best, we head out like an ancient mariner clutching a map with only this direction: *That way dragons be.*

3

KANSAS, 1912

My mom was born in the tiny town of Oketo, Kansas, eight years before women's suffrage. It was the summer of 1912, and the White House was occupied by the forgettable William Howard Taft. A few months later, much to the pleasure of Adelaide's father—who was a county school superintendent and a progressive—Woodrow Wilson would be elected. Wilson was an academic, a former president of Princeton University, and a Democrat.

Wilson's presidency wouldn't fulfill my grandfather's expectations, but his daughter would. Throughout her life, she maintained an unswaying allegiance to the importance of education, the righteousness of liberal politics, and a preference for the company of smart men. They would remain the guiding stars of her life.

When Adelaide was a little girl, she loved to take tests. She liked to tell the story of how she and her younger sister Stella Marie—known as Tudie for reasons no one could ever explain—were disappointed when they finished taking an early version of the IQ test. The test was fun, they thought. They just wished it had gone on longer.

The test Adelaide and her sister would likely have taken was the one developed by Dr. Lewis Terman, who introduced the American version of the IQ test in 1916. He called it the Stanford–Binet Intelligence Scales—a nod to the French inventor of the IQ test, and to the university where Terman would become famous, and where Adelaide would eventually make her home.

✦

Not only was her father the county school superintendent, her mother was a former teacher. Adelaide and her three sisters received their early lessons at home, and Adelaide did not attend school until she entered second grade one year early, at the age of six. Around that same time, the family was forced to move. My grandparents were of Luxembourger descent, but Schmitt sounded suspiciously German at the onset of World War I, and his name cost my grandfather his job.

They lived in several small Kansas towns before settling in Lawrence, where my grandfather was a school principal and could work on his master's degree while he and Adelaide developed their mutual devotion to college sports by attending Kansas University games. From that point forward, my grandfather would pen a song for each new school he served, all to the tune of "Crimson and Blue," the Kansas alma mater.

My grandfather owned a car well before it was commonplace, and in his third daughter, Adelaide, he found an eager passenger. He taught her to drive when she was fourteen, and together they bounced around the Kansas countryside on what passed for roads, imprinting on my mom a love for car travel she never lost. For her, a map and a car equaled happiness.

She felt the same way about sports, but unlike her older sister Agnes, she wasn't a born athlete. She always attributed her lack of athletic prowess to a broken wrist that hadn't been set properly when she was a school girl. But the truth is, she never believed in excessive outdoor activity.

Later in life, some of her best friends had a lunch badminton club. Adelaide met them for the meal but never played, just as she never learned how to swim or take part in any other sport. Athletics was the only arena where she preferred observation to participation. But oh how she loved the action. It was here. It was now. It was live. And so was she.

In the late 1930s, when Adelaide was still in her twenties, she and her sister Agnes headed out on a cross-country road trip. And not just across the United States. The two of them drove unaccompanied, all the way across Mexico, too. I suspect my grandfather was a bit envious, but he must have also been pleased by their adventurousness. He'd always encouraged his daughters' independence and inquisitiveness. Every week, he brought home a new book for each of his girls. He would have been pleased, I think, that over a hundred years later, several of those books, like the 1917 edition of Thorton Burgess's *The Adventures of Paddy the Beaver*, now occupy the bookshelves of his great-great-grandchildren.

My grandparents didn't only place their faith in education and liberal politics, they were also devout Catholics. And according to family lore, that adherence to Catholicism and priestly authority accounted for the names of the first two Schmitt girls. When it came time to baptize their first child, the story goes, my grandparents dutifully brought their baby girl to church for the ceremony.

The parish priest began by saying, "Today is the feast day of St. Cecilia. And in the Name of the Father, the Son and the Holy Ghost, I baptize thee Cecelia."

It was not the name my grandparents had intended, but Cecelia she became.

The same thing happened when their second daughter was born. This time, the priest began by saying, "Today is the feast day of St. Agnes...and so I baptize thee Agnes."

But by child number three, my grandfather was not to be denied. It was now 1912, after all. She would be named Adelaide, and Adelaide she would always be.

Adelaide and her three sisters thrived in school and school-related competitions, none of the sisters evidencing much interest in anything domestic. My mom graduated early from both high school and college. One of her sisters became an accomplished poet, another a recreational therapist for the Red Cross, another a high school administrator. Adelaide, not surprisingly, became a teacher. She was a committed educator who wouldn't get married until she was in her early thirties—by which time, she liked to say, she still didn't know how to fry an egg.

4

DAY TO DAY

Fall 2008

MY MOM AND I BOTH LOVED THE FALL. Even in the temperate Bay Area, you could build a fire, watch football, and find an excuse to bundle up.

Not surprisingly, my mom had a full sweatshirt collection representing every university anyone in her family had ever attended, including one for her own alma mater, the University of Michigan. And one day, in the fall of 2008, I found her in the TV room, sporting a dark-blue pullover with a gold MICHIGAN emblazoned across the chest. But she wasn't watching the maize and blue compete on the gridiron. She was on the phone, engaged in her other favorite fall pastime: politics. And she was in fine form.

My mom was a huge Barack Obama fan, and the presidential election of 2008 was fast approaching. I'd arranged to have her make phone calls from home, on behalf of his candidacy, but she didn't stick fully to the prescribed script, beginning each call like this instead: "Hello. My name is Adelaide Iverson. I'm ninety-six years old, and we've just lived through the worst president in my lifetime. So I'd like you to support Barack Obama."

Adelaide Iverson's passions, from community concerns to the Stanford Cardinal, were always focused on the present moment, and on what she hoped the future could become. Over the course of her long life, she'd taught school, registered voters, tutored women inmates at the county jail, and gone door-to-door to support the candidates and causes she championed. In short, she always supported her teams. She believed she could make a difference in multiple arenas. And she did.

My mom always said that she was proudest of her work at the county jail, where she helped women inmates prepare for the high school equivalency exam. I think she liked the direct connection between teaching and a concrete outcome. But she also liked doing it because of what it taught her, including an expansion of her vocabulary.

My mom always wanted to look her best, and dressed accordingly, no matter where she was headed. One day, upon arriving at the jail, a young woman greeted her by saying, "Mrs. Iverson, you look *bad* today!"

She was flummoxed until her student assured her that *bad* actually meant *good*.

My mom loved telling that story, though she never quite succeeded in giving *bad* the right inflection.

✦

That fall marked the end of our first year together, and among the many things I'd already learned was the importance of scheduling. Because if the caregiving calendar falls apart, you do, too.

Like many caregivers, Mele worked two jobs, taking care of another client at night. That meant she had to leave before I got home from work. My mom seemed comfortable being home alone for that amount of time, but if I had to work late or go out of town, the gaps got trickier to fill. My younger brother, Paul, and his wife, Yoko, lived nearby, and they would often stop by to make sure everything was OK. I'd recruit Mele's mother or Yoko to stay overnight if need be. And I'd ask neighbors or some of my mom's younger friends (meaning those in their seventies or eighties) to come by for an hour, here or there. When I was out of town, I'd create schedules that were as intricate as a house of cards—and about as stable.

One day, when I was late getting home from work, I found my mom sitting on the living room floor. She'd fallen and hadn't been able to get up. She was fine, though. In fact, she was sitting there reading *The New York Times*. But a fall gets your attention. I knew I needed to reduce the amount of time she was home alone, but I also wanted to hang on to what independence I could. So I just made an incremental scheduling change.

I don't recall any additional falls, and I probably got some mileage out of telling the story about my mom reading the newspaper on the floor, but my journal entries from earlier in the year reveal that my life as a caregiver was starting to shift in a new direction.

✦

I have to be ready for each day
and not get upset that we keep

going over the same thing. I can't
let that get to me.

Sometimes I have that proverbial
"last straw" reaction where
I'm on the edge of anger and
frustration. I have to act like
Mom and I have never had this
conversation before.

—May 17, 2008

Reading my old journal entries was a reminder that, while my mom might be a marvel, I was beginning to struggle with some of caregiving's daily demands. In this case, what I felt were my mom's repetitive comments or complaints. I was used to being able to charm my mom, to make her smile. And while we could have great fun together, I couldn't smooth every bump in her day, or in mine. I was holding my own at work—hosting my radio show and starting work on a new documentary—but I was coming home to a different reality. We were both used to getting our way and realizing that sometimes we couldn't.

There's nothing novel about that; it's just how caregiving is.

A sports cliché often used to describe an injured player's status is that he or she is day-to-day. But as the iconic sportscaster Vin Scully once observed, "Aren't we all day-to-day?"

When you're a caregiver, the person you take care of is day-to-day. But so are you. In fact, caregiving may be one of life's ultimate day-to-day enterprises. And part of what makes the job challenging is that you don't get to choose whether to go out onto the playing field. The starting buzzer always sounds.

✦

> I feel weary. Even sitting here
> right now, I just feel weary.
>
> My biggest challenge right now
> is to feel that I'm in charge of my
> life, rather than being captured
> by circumstance.
>
> —May 4, 2008

✦

I don't know what triggered that bout of malaise, but my bet is, nothing much. The day happened, that's all. Something reminded me that I wasn't fully in charge of my life, and that momentary reality was wearing me out. But it also wouldn't surprise me if later that same day, I spent a few satisfying hours working on my new film, or went to a Stanford game where my mom and I cheered our heads off. A central caregiving reality is that you can experience love and loss, frustration and fulfillment, usually when weary, and often on the same day.

All of this just means that even before I hit the one-year mark in my caregiving experience, I was beginning to realize that along with its rewards, helping my mom might get a whole lot more challenging than I'd initially thought. But I also think that in order to do what caregiving requires, starting out with a certain amount of wishful thinking, or even willful ignorance, has its advantages.

I'd begun my caregiving stint with faith in the strength of our relationship, and faith in my own ability to sail through what lay ahead, including my own Parkinson's diagnosis. If that means I was compartmentalizing, or engaging in denial, it's also true that deploying that approach enabled me to get on with the tasks at hand. It's what allowed me to stay in motion when a sober, clear-eyed view of reality might not have. The utility of a good rationalization shouldn't be underestimated.

I also think this may be why some caregivers—especially those who care for spouses—deny that they're caregivers at all. I'm sure my mom would never have described herself as a caregiver during my dad's final years.

"Bill is my husband," she would have said. "And I'm his wife. Period."

I would have rejected that label early on as well. I was just there to lend a helping hand for what I thought was a limited-time arrangement. If I'd been more deliberative about my decision to move in, I would likely have come to the rueful realization that nothing in my mom's life had *ever* suggested her final years would transpire along some gentle glide path followed by a soft landing. She was never going to "go gently into that good night."

But of course, I didn't think it through that thoroughly, and I'm glad I didn't. Because otherwise, I might not have done it.

How's that for a rationalization?

+

As Christmas of 2008 approached, life with my mom seemed to be shifting once more. She'd always loved Christmas and all the preparation that went with it. She had particularly strong opinions about Christmas trees, and ever since I'd moved back to California, it had been our annual ritual to go select a tree together. I would come down from San Francisco and take her to the same lot where the proceeds benefited the local Kiwanis club, a cause she supported. We'd walk slowly up and down the aisles until she spotted just the right one.

But this year, she couldn't use her walker well enough to get out and look around. In recent days, she seemed less herself, more confused, and—most concerning—less interested in the world around her. She didn't even seem excited that she'd soon have a new president.

+

> I was up with Mom five times during the night.
>
> This isn't her fault. I have to be patient. Whatever is happening isn't in her control.
>
> —December 21, 2008

+

Sitting by the fireplace in the evening that Christmas, I tried reading aloud excerpts from Doris Kearns Goodwin's book *No Ordinary Time*, about Franklin and Eleanor Roosevelt. I read to my mom about the era that had spanned my parents' passionate romance and lengthy separation, but reading brought little response. I took her temperature and she didn't have a fever. She just seemed disconnected and so very, very tired.

✛

Late at night, Adelaide keeps asking, "What's happening?" and "When did this happen?"

—December 26, 2008

✛

I had solo duty the day after Christmas, and I remember standing by her bed and asking, "Can you tell me what's wrong, Mom?"

She couldn't answer, but she must have had some sense that her ability to keep everything straight had at least temporarily gone missing. Nor could she let it go and just rest. She'd mutter and turn her head and struggle for words, as if part of her brain was still poking around, trying this synapse and then another, looking for the right connection but finding only dead ends and broken wiring. And yet the elemental Adelaide was unwilling to let go, determined to try to figure out what in the world was happening to her.

Later that same evening, I wanted to get outside and go for a run, but I worried about leaving my mom alone. So I did a half-mile loop around the neighborhood, then jogged back up the front walk into the house, and entered my mom's room to look in on her. Then I'd head back outside for another loop, and then another jog-by check-in, until I'd finally done my three miles.

By the next day, her decline was even more noticeable. She was struggling to use the walker and get to the bathroom in time. Independence, I remember thinking, is really just a matter of inches.

And she was no longer always making sense. "Wrinkle," she would say. Then, "Open it," and, "White cotton jacket." That lively, remarkable brain of hers was growing cloudier, seemingly by the hour.

I called the doctor, who asked me to bring her in. I grimaced, knowing how arduous that would be. But she was docile, perhaps the most telling sign yet that something was wrong.

Dr. Margaret Forsyth had been her physician for many years, and I could tell how concerned she was that this new persona had replaced the Adelaide she'd always known. Later that night, she called to say that Adelaide's white blood count was sky high, indicating some sort of infection. And since it was Friday night, I should take her to the ER the next morning.

Lynn and I had planned to take Adelaide to Asilomar, a favorite family spot near Carmel, along the California coast, for the New Year's holiday weekend. But now we had a different destination. The trip to the ER was uneventful, and a lab test established that she had a major urinary tract infection—the dreaded UTI. The doctor put her on IV antibiotics but also indicated that the infection might only be exacerbating a more general decline. I shouldn't hope for dramatic improvement.

After my mom was moved to her own room, I settled in to sit with her for a few hours before heading home. As my mom slept, I visited quietly with a nursing assistant named Gerri and told her the basics of Adelaide's story— her age, her remarkable life and fierce independence, and my decision to move in with her the year before. She listened thoughtfully and then said, "Love between a parent and a child never ends. That connection is always there, even when that person no longer is."

Gerri was middle-aged, younger than I was but not by much. She went on to tell me that her own daughter had died a few years before at the age of twenty-three.

"She's always with me. I feel her with me every day."

The hospital stay was long and arduous. The UTI proved to be a tough matchup for whatever drugs the doctors selected, and the overall hospital experience was profoundly disorienting. Nights were especially tough. My niece Erika flew out from New York to see her, and she'd spend the night with her grandmother at the hospital. She told me that my mom would sometimes engage in extended dreamlike discourses during the night, but that the essential Grandma Adelaide was still present.

"Erika," my mom told her one night, "If this goes on much longer it may do serious damage to our relationship."

After twelve long days and longer nights, the IV antibiotics eventually won out, and my mom was transferred to a nearby skilled nursing center for additional convalescence and rehabilitation. That's when a remarkable woman entered our lives.

✦

Walking into the lobby of the skilled nursing facility felt like entering the lobby of an upscale hotel, and in an odd way was even more disconcerting than walking into an old-fashioned nursing home.

I remembered what it felt like to enter the place where my dad had spent the last fifteen months of his life. I didn't sense much warmth, and it sure didn't convey a feeling of home. But at least it was what it was: a place that provided a clean, if bleak, setting for those who would either recover and go home, or would live out the rest of their lives receiving kind and efficient care.

But when I stepped into this place, I wasn't sure where I was. There was soft, piped-in music. Or perhaps it was the manufactured sounds of a bubbling brook. I don't recall. There were flowers and hotel art. It was all carpeted, neatly kept, and carefully presented. Was it really filled with people drifting between life and death?

My mom's room was just as well-appointed, though she was far from appreciative. She wasn't happy—something she made clear to whoever walked through the door to assist her.

Within a few days, a nursing assistant by the name of Eileen Khan seemed to take over as Adelaide's primary care provider. Only later did I learn that Eileen was there not by routine assignment, but by default. She was the only one who had the chops to deal with a bedridden, but by no means docile, Adelaide Iverson. Within forty-eight hours, word had apparently gone out among the staff: Watch out for the woman in room 103. She may be approaching a hundred, but she can be holy hell.

Eileen was from Fiji originally, and because of the high cost of housing in the Bay Area, she lived nearly two hours away, on the edge of California's Central Valley. Later, I would learn that she only made it home to see her three kids on the weekends, spending weeknights sleeping on the floor at her parents' nearby apartment.

Eileen was not only highly skilled, she had an easy air of self-confidence, and a keen but kindly eye. She quickly sized up my mom. Eileen seemed to know that having a successful relationship with Adelaide required an ability to go eyeball to eyeball as equals. My mom despised condescension, but she had an equally fierce response to timidity. Now, someone who strode into the room with confidence, humor, and a bit of hubris? Well, let the games begin.

But for all my mom's ferocity of spirit, her body was now less resilient. Just a few nights before she was transferred from the hospital, she'd tried to climb out of her bed and had fallen to the floor. But as was customary for someone who seemed impervious to pain, she appeared to survive the tumble without any harm. But less than a week into her rehabilitation stay, she was still unable to step forward. The physical therapist suspected something was wrong with her left ankle, and in fact, it was broken. My mom would be in a cast and wheelchair for the remainder of her stay at the nursing home, and for several weeks once she returned home.

I knew this development meant that I would need more help. As great as Mele was, she was only able to provide thirty-five hours a week of daytime help, and that wasn't going to be enough now that my mom was more needy. I asked Eileen if she'd be interested in an extra part-time job. When she said yes, I felt like I'd won the lottery.

After a fourteen-day stay, Adelaide was discharged. Before heading home, both Mele and I received training on how to transfer my mom from bed to wheelchair to commode and back again. Mele and Eileen were big, strong women, both six feet tall. I felt wimpy by comparison at five-foot-nine, but learning the right technique helped me accomplish what was necessary.

In the months ahead, I'd sometimes joke that if I ever needed extra work I'd now be able to get a job at a home care agency. But in reality, I'd only mastered a fraction of what that profession demands.

✦

Our first year together had come to a close, and my mom's hospitalization was a reminder of both her increasing vulnerability and her remarkable staying power. Her life story was going to continue, but I wasn't sure in what form. People liked to call her a force of nature, and until now, she'd always managed to remain at the center of the action. She was the ninety-six-year-old who not only cheered at games, but made calls for candidates. She could still be, and often was, the life of the party. As a close friend of mine once put it, "Adelaide should rent herself out for special occasions."

Of course, you never knew exactly how those evenings would unfold—like the time I took her to my closest friend's home to celebrate the Seder. We were in the middle of telling the Passover story when she interrupted to make sure all the guests knew that some of her best friends were Jewish. But that was the thing about my mom. You always knew she was in the room.

And now I wondered what lay ahead. Whether she'd retain that same forceful presence and that same remarkable voice—its spark, as well as its singe.

5

DEAR ADELAIDE

Fall, 1946

FIFTEEN MONTHS AFTER THE END OF WORLD WAR II, an eager 35 year old Army veteran named Bill Iverson arrived on the Stanford University campus. He'd been accepted at Stanford's Graduate School of Education, where Lewis Terman, the legendary creator of the American IQ test, still held forth. For Bill, it meant the resumption of his educational dream—a dream deferred twice before.

He'd grown up poor in Buffalo, New York, the oldest child of Norwegian and English immigrants. He was an excellent student, so promising that his high school principal tutored him in Latin and Greek before school each day in order to increase Bill's chances of becoming the first in his family to attend college. But a year after he started at the University of Buffalo, the Great Depression took hold and his dad lost his job at a local steel mill. So Bill dropped out of college to support his parents and three younger siblings.

Putting the acting skills he'd honed in high school to work, he landed a job in local radio, where he did everything from hosting a children's story hour to acting in the first radio drama versions of *The Lone Ranger* and *The Green Hornet*, penned by fellow Buffalo native Fran Striker. It wasn't until he was in his mid-twenties that Bill was able to return to college, eventually transferring to the University of Michigan and graduating in 1938. His Michigan professors encouraged him to go to graduate school, but he needed to make money first, and started teaching at a nearby junior high school.

Two years later, with war imminent, Bill was drafted into the US Army. His teaching career at Grosse Pointe's Pierce Junior High School may have been cut short in 1940, but by then, the popular young drama teacher, and a striking but stern history teacher named Adelaide Schmitt, had become an item. Bill would spend the next six years in the Army, but despite long separations, he and Adelaide still managed to marry during the war. And in 1944, Adelaide gave birth to their first child, Peter. Finally, with the war over, life could begin anew. With high hopes, they headed for California.

Bill and Adelaide and two-year-old Peter settled into what was euphemistically known as Stanford Village, a series of ramshackle buildings that had served as a military hospital during the war, and now provided housing for married graduate students and junior faculty. Their apartment happened to be next to those of several aspiring physicists and their families, including two future Nobel laureates. That accidental association forged lifelong friendships. Those same couples—the

Hofstadters, the Chodorows, the Schiffs, and many more—would wind up spending almost every Fourth of July, election night, and New Year's Eve together for the next forty years—a bond strengthened by shared post-war dreams and the arrival of new offspring.

In the fall of 1948, while still living in Stanford Village, Bill and Adelaide were expecting their second child. Bill borrowed a car so they'd be able to make the trip to the hospital, but he wasn't exactly mechanical, and when Adelaide went into labor, starting a balky car was apparently beyond him. Their next-door neighbor, Leonard Schiff—who would one day chair the Stanford Physics Department—heard the ruckus and yelled out the window to see if he could help. Leonard got the car started, and I was born at Stanford Hospital a few hours later.

Stanford Village was also home to the Stanford University Nursery School, where Lewis Terman's disciples continued his long-term study of childhood intelligence. My mom enrolled me when I was two, and I later became a study subject and the taker of many tests. I turned out to be another kid who liked taking exams and talking about the results—an example of an apple that hadn't fallen too far from the tree, as illustrated by an exchange my mom loved to recount.

"Mom," I said, looking up at her one day, when I was a little boy. "We sure like ourselves, don't we?"

I started life in the kind of worry-free household that many parents of that era tried to make possible. Having lived through both the Depression and World War II, I suspect nothing mattered more to them than creating a steadying environment. So when the Stanford School of Education offered my dad a faculty position in 1950, my parents swallowed their financial anxieties and placed a down payment on what would turn out to be the only home they'd ever know: a brand-new, fifteen-hundred-square-foot ranch-style home in nearby Menlo Park. It was purchased for, what seemed to them, the astronomical price of $15,000.

My younger brother, Paul, was born a few years later, and my two brothers and I grew up in a quintessential post-war 1950s neighborhood where everything had its place, including a fundamental separation between the lives of children and their parents. The era of chummy parent-child chats and shared pursuits was a long ways away. We knew what was expected of us, and we knew what to expect of them. As boys, we were to be courteous, kind, and well-behaved, and our parents would be exactly the same. It didn't occur to us that we ought to know more about our parents' lives.

As the novelist Richard Ford observed in his memoir about his parents, *Between Them*: "Incomplete understanding of our parents' lives is not a condition of their lives. Only ours. If anything, to realize we know less than all is respectful, since children narrow the frame of everything they're part of."

But even as we carried out the separate business of sibling life, I think my brothers and I did understand something fundamental about our family. We weren't the center of our parents' lives; they were. And that essential truth provided clarity and orderliness to our family life.

✦

It wasn't until I was in my late thirties and my father's

health began to decline, that I gained a keener appreciation of who my parents really were to each other. My dad was diagnosed with Parkinson's when he was turning sixty, and he did reasonably well for the next fifteen years. But his final years were increasingly difficult, and my mom provided a lasting example of what true love entails. She was by his side every moment. And when he finally had to be moved to a long-term care facility, she was there every day, dressed to the nines and making sure my dad received the best care.

"That is not how you comb his hair," she would sternly command. "You comb it like this."

She was especially tough on anyone who didn't talk to my dad as the man she knew him to be. Parkinson's had limited his ability to move and speak, but not who he was.

"You do *not* call him sweetie, and you do *not* call him Bill," she would tell whoever was assisting him. "You call him Dr. Iverson."

She was a commanding figure, no doubt striking terror in the attending staff. I used to wonder if someone got on the intercom and issued an alert whenever my mom was spotted arriving in the parking lot.

By the end of my dad's life, he could usually only say a few words at a time, but he could still make those words count. I remember sitting with him late one night, when he motioned me over to his bedside. I leaned in close to make sure I heard him.

He looked at me and said, "You're getting really gray."

At the time, it wasn't the classic father-son moment I was expecting, but now I realize it was exactly that—a gentle poke well-delivered, revealing a subtle slyness I didn't know he had.

A few months later, I flew back from my home in the Midwest to visit him again. In his last years, he had mild Parkinson's-related dementia and would get disoriented at night. On the last evening of my visit, I read to him from a book about his native Buffalo, and then told him that I had to fly home the next day. He looked around the room, then reached for a tissue.

He held it up and said, "Can you use this to pay for the ticket?"

I think those were the last words he ever said to me— kindly and courteous to the end.

My dad passed away a few weeks later. And when I flew back for the memorial, I stayed at my parents' home, as I always did. The night before the service, my mom tapped on the door of the bedroom where I'd slept as a boy. She came in and handed me a billfold—the slim, vertical, old-fashioned kind that you keep in the inside pocket of a suit coat. She'd given it to my dad the night before they got married in 1942. On that September night, fifty-two years before, she'd placed a note inside the billfold that my dad carried with him the rest of his life. I had never opened that billfold before, or known of the note's existence.

I unfolded it slowly, and this is what I read:

> Dear Bill,
>
> I love you. It will take me the rest of my life to show you how much.
>
> —Adelaide

Those words, and the ones my dad had spoken to me during my final visits with him, seemed to embody who my parents were: careful and caring, tender and spare. No need to say more than necessary, especially about anything personal.

But a few months after my dad died, when I was going through some of his old files, I came across a box of letters pushed back under his desk. The letters were piled haphazardly, hundreds of them, all written by my dad during his six-year stint in the Army, when my parents had mostly lived apart. My mom had apparently saved every one. And just like the note my mom had tucked inside that billfold, I had never seen any of the letters before.

I started reading.

+

Summer, 1940

Dear Adelaide,

Be prepared to be trampled in the rush of my greeting when we meet next. I am going to overwhelm you as no woman has ever been overwhelmed before. I think I'll shout and leap into the air. Throw my hat down and stomp on it. Seize you and fling you over my shoulder. Gallop madly down the street...to the hotel.

—Bill

So much for spare and tender. It's not that I thought of my parents as austere, but they'd always carried themselves with such rectitude. Despite their deep affection for each other, they'd seemed relentlessly proper, and my father in particular had always been a buttoned-down, tucked-in kind of fellow.

Really? I remember thinking. *Dad?*

But as I read one letter after another, a different man emerged—alternatingly bawdy and poetic, rueful about the state of the world, and savage in his skewering of the Army. And what shone through most was his passion for my mom.

✦

Fall, 1940

Dear Adelaide,

The rest of today's training is to be devoted to organized athletics.
I am organizing my own games on the bunk. Would you like to join me?

—Bill

✦

I remember sitting there in my dad's old study, shaking my head, surrounded by the shelves of sober books he'd penned, and a pile of penciled letters stacked beside me.

My mom had told occasional stories about this other Bill Iverson, the glib former radio actor she'd first met at Pierce Junior High. And she relished saying how she hadn't thought much of him at first.

"He was just too loud," she'd say. "Too much of a showoff."

And I think my brothers and I just assumed that she'd been the one to button him down and shape him into the kindly, professorial man we knew. For us, she was always the more formidable of the two, and it wasn't hard for us to imagine her primly presiding over ninth grade history class and not giving that loudmouth down the hall the time of day.

But then I thought about another story my mom loved to tell. One day, in history class, she'd intercepted a note two girls were passing back and forth. After class, she unfolded it and read: "Honestly, what in the world does that dreamy Mr. Iverson see in Miss Schmitt????"

And then my mom would laugh and tell us how popular Bill Iverson had been with all the females—faculty and students alike.

I was starting to wonder—maybe it wasn't my mom who'd tamed my dad. Maybe my dad had unbuttoned my mom a bit as well.

+

Fall, 1941

Dear Adelaide,

You don't wear sheer blouses?

Pity.

—Bill

+

I wish I knew how my mom responded to that imagery, but I only found one wartime letter of hers. It was sweetly affectionate, fondly chiding my dad for the amount of weight he'd gained since their previous hotel rendezvous. It was a letter she'd never mailed, but it must have been an observation she'd offered frequently, given my dad's subsequent acknowledgement:

"Yes," he wrote, "I got folds of flesh like a tired accordion."

This was an era when long-distance phone calls were still considered an extravagance—one my dad didn't think he could afford on his infantryman's paycheck. And so they wrote almost daily, with my dad often plaintively noting how much he longed for the next letter, and how bereft he was when one didn't arrive. They were separated by time and space in a way that I don't think I could ever have fully comprehended, save for that box of letters. "I want to talk to you in all the odd moments," he once wrote. "The even ones will take care of themselves."

My dad hated the Army. In his telling, he was perhaps the least able soldier ever, routinely making a mess of everything from rifle practice to marching. After one particularly notable performance on the shooting range, his bewildered company commander asked him, "How can anyone shoot that way?" Nor was he any better when sent out on reconnaissance, once writing my mom: "Give me a map, and I get lost. Give me a map and a compass, and I get lost completely. Give me a map, compass, and binoculars, and I'm gone for days."

Despite his ineptitude, he felt there was one military option he had to pursue. He wrote my mom a lengthy letter explaining that he didn't feel they could get married unless he could boost his infantryman's pay. So in the spring of 1942, he applied to Officers Candidate School, knowing that if he was accepted, his tour of duty would likely be extended.

He got in—a feat my father took as further testimony to the Army's incompetence—and by September of 1942, Lieutenant William Iverson had scraped together enough cash and time off to go back to Grosse Pointe, Michigan, and get married.

Perhaps because he displayed less than stellar military prowess, my dad managed to stay out of harm's way throughout World War II, serving stateside as a supply officer at various Army bases in California and the Northwest for the remainder of his service. Except for occasional visits, my parents were apart for the duration of the war. "I hate trains that leave," he wrote. "Trains should only arrive."

The only time they would live together during his six years in the service occurred as the war was coming to an end. It turned out that my dad had been right—being an officer kept him in the Army for an additional year, until the summer of 1946. But he was one of the lucky ones and he knew it.

I sat in his old study for hours, reading what my dad had written fifty years before. The war had cost them time, but not their future. His delicate penciled script had faded, but the love he described never did.

+

Spring, 1942

Dear Adelaide,

Sometimes I think our love is to
be tried many times...and that
out of trying times may come
a timeless purity which we will
always hold in our hearts.

—Bill

6

A FAMILY CONDITION

Summer, 1971

MY DAD MAY HAVE BEEN A FORMER RADIO ACTOR, but he never seemed to seek center stage. He was a "no fuss, no muss" kind of guy—disinclined to call attention to himself, and definitely not one to provoke alarm. So it wasn't surprising that I received news about his health from my mom, not him. And she delivered it in her usual matter-of-fact manner.

It was the summer of 1971, and following college graduation, I'd joined VISTA—Volunteers in Service to America—which was like a domestic version of the Peace Corps. I was assigned to a project in Richmond, Indiana, and I remember opening my mom's letter while standing in front of the kitchen sink. My mom began with the usual pleasantries and then got down to business. "Your dad," she wrote, "has been diagnosed with Parkinson's disease."

I didn't even know what those words meant, nor did she offer any further information. So I rummaged around for a dictionary, then read this definition for the first time: "Parkinson's: a progressive, neurodegenerative disease for which there is no cure."

But when I saw my dad a few months later, he seemed unchanged. He was still on the faculty at Stanford's School of Education—by now, a noted specialist in the teaching of reading and children's literature—and he was giving a lecture at nearby Dayton University. As usual, he didn't talk about himself much, only surreptitiously slipping a new pill out of his pocket to take at mealtime. We spent a pleasant weekend together, and after he left, I did what you do when you're twenty-two: I didn't think about it that much.

The new medication he was taking turned out to be a breakthrough Parkinson's drug that had just come on the market, and treated the more pronounced symptoms of the disease. And just as important, my dad would have the active, relentless support of my mom. She wasn't about to alter their overall approach to life, or the activities she'd inked in on her calendar—no pencil for her. Sometimes people were perplexed by her business-like attitude, sensing a lack of compassion. But her approach, I would learn, made sense.

Years later, my cousin Peter would tell me that when he was treating people with Parkinson's in his physical therapy practice, he would often cite my mom's approach. He believed that her no-nonsense, no-giving-in demeanor—coupled with her devotion to my dad—was the model approach for spouses of Parkinson's patients.

Expecting my dad to put on his own coat wasn't being hard-hearted. It just meant that they had a game to get to and they'd best get on with it.

With few exceptions, my mom was not inclined to either dwell on life's challenges or be depressed by them. Her basic approach to life with Parkinson's was similar to how she would later approach her own old age: why in the world should life change just because you're getting old? It turns out that a little bit of denial can go a long way.

My parents took longer to do things, but they still did them. They just got to Stanford basketball games early and left late. They still attended the same New Year's Eve and election night parties with the same Stanford Village crowd. They never talked with their friends about my dad's Parkinson's; they just kept moving forward. And staying in motion matters with Parkinson's, a condition that tends to take things from you, one movement at a time. An arm no longer swings, a step becomes a shuffle— it's a disease of subtle subtraction. My parents were the first to show me that if you keep adding to your life, you can extend your stay on the plus side of the ledger.

Over the long run, though, Parkinson's usually exacts an inexorable toll. Medication helps with the symptoms, but it doesn't alter the fundamental course. By the mid-1980s, fifteen years after his diagnosis, the rate of my dad's decline began to accelerate. I was still living in the Midwest, and during one of my periodic visits back to California, I had a chance to talk with his neurologist. He assured me that my dad was doing as well as could be expected, and then he said, "You know, you and your brothers don't have to worry about getting Parkinson's. It isn't genetic."

✦

Six years later, in the early 1990s, I got a call from my older brother. Peter was a distinguished professor of history at Arizona State University, and his career was thriving. He seemed to always have a new book in the works, but he'd called to talk about something entirely different. He'd been having tingling sensations in his left hand and foot. He wasn't sure what was going on, and neither were the doctors, but he was concerned and wondered if he might be experiencing Parkinson's early symptoms.

There's no biological test or imaging technique that yields a definitive diagnosis of Parkinson's—no MRI, biopsy, or blood test. A Parkinson's assessment is based on a skilled neurologist's observations, often over a period of time.

A few months later, my brother wrote me a short letter. All it said was, "I got the diagnosis. And I have Parkinson's." He was just forty-eight years old.

✦

A dozen years later, in 2003, I was working at my desk in San Francisco one afternoon when I felt my cell phone vibrating in my left front pants pocket. I reached for it, but as I pulled the phone out, I saw there wasn't a call after all. I didn't think anything of it initially, but I continued to experience the same phantom sensation in the month that followed, along with an odd vibrating sensation in my left arm. It felt like my arm was trembling on the inside, even though the outside remained perfectly still. I wouldn't normally have worried about such minor, curious symptoms, but now there was history, and I couldn't help but wonder if it was my turn.

A few days later, while out walking in my San Francisco neighborhood, I noticed my left arm wasn't swinging quite the same as my right. It brought me up short. One of my dad's first symptoms was losing his left arm swing. I tried to figure out if what I thought I was seeing was actually real. Maybe it was just in my head. Maybe my antenna was way too finely tuned. I'd try to measure my arm swing while I walked down the street, switching whatever I happened to be carrying—a bag of groceries or a water bottle—from one hand to the other to try to see if my free hand swung differently. My left arm always swung less.

I decided to call my internist, a perceptive physician who had the unusual attribute of always returning your calls, usually late at night. Around 11:30 p.m. the next night, the phone rang.

"This is Phil O'Keefe," he said. "Tell me what's going on."

I filled in more detail, and then he said, "I want to see you. Come into the office tomorrow."

The next afternoon, he put me through an extensive exam, checking my flexibility, muscle tone, balance, gait, and mobility. And when he was done, he looked me in the eye and said, "You'll need to see a specialist, but I think you might well have Parkinson's."

I shouldn't have been shocked, but I was floored.

A few hours later, I was riding on the light rail line

near my apartment when it came to a sudden stop. We all staggered to keep our balance, and as I looked around, who did I see but my doctor, standing just ten feet away.

He regarded me with a wry smile and said, "Balance. Remember, from now on, it's all about balance."

Over the next few days, I called Lynn, then my daughter, Laura, and then Peter. Lynn was up in the High Sierra, at a friend's cabin.

"I'll be right there," she said.

When I called Laura, she burst into tears, but when it was time for me to see a specialist a month later, she flew out from Boston to be with me. It was only when I called my older brother, Peter, that I got a little choked up.

"We'll just have to fight this together," he said.

It would be another year before the diagnosis was confirmed, but I've always remembered those conversations and what my doctor said that first afternoon: "Balance. It's all about balance."

$$\text{---}\!\!+\!\!\text{---}$$

The day after my doctor's first tentative diagnosis, I joined my neighborhood gym. I had no idea whether exercise would be helpful to managing Parkinson's. I just knew that I wanted to feel like I was still in control of my body.

I started lifting weights for the first time in my life. I worked on core strengthening, which I had always hated, and found I still did, proving that Parkinson's doesn't change everything. And while I'd been an occasional jogger, I now started running consistently. I remember feeling determined, though I can't say what I felt determined about.

I was fifty-six years old and had been a journalist almost all my professional life, which carries with it a certain occupational hazard. You tend to see the world through the lens of story possibilities. You notice an emerging phenomenon, whether it's the surprising popularity of an unsung candidate, or an unsung vegetable like kale, and wonder what the story is behind it. And sometimes you look at what's going on in your own life that way, too. It wasn't long before I began to think about my family story and whether it might provide the platform to explore the broader questions surrounding Parkinson's disease, a condition that was in the crosshairs of the ongoing societal debate over fetal tissue transplants and stem cell research.

There's a certain self-indulgent quality to this, of course: because it's happening to you, it must be important. I'd never done a story before from a first-person perspective, but this felt different.

Over the next two and a half years, my symptoms continued to be mild. I was able to pursue the idea of making a film about Parkinson's, while working on other projects and hosting my weekly radio show. And then, in the late spring of 2007, I got two phone calls. One from the MacArthur Foundation, telling me I'd been awarded a major grant, another giving me the greenlight and additional funding to make the film for the PBS *Frontline* series. The film would explore the societal and scientific dilemmas posed by Parkinson's, as well as my family's journey with the disease. It would be titled *My Father, My Brother and Me.*

A few months later, in the fall of 2007, I moved in with my mom.

✦

I realize that the timing of my decision to become a caregiver seems like a head-scratcher. Even if I was doing well, how could I have decided to move in and take care of my mom only a few years after being diagnosed with Parkinson's? And not only that, I knew something about what lay in store. I'd seen how Parkinson's had affected my dad, and how it was currently impacting my brother. And here I was adding my own little twist to our family story: a person with Parkinson's choosing to take care of someone else. What was I thinking? Or perhaps more to the point, what was I *not* thinking about?

Sometimes I've wondered if I was just following my mom's example, opting for a little utilitarian denial rather than focusing on the long-term prognosis. There's nothing like finding a new way to be extra busy to take your mind off an unpleasant reality. Of course, the beauty of denial is that you don't know you're in denial, but I don't think that fully explains my decision.

The truth is, not only was I doing well, my Parkinson's symptoms were almost imperceptible. The standard Parkinson's medications worked well for me, and I was now fitter and stronger than I'd ever been. I felt pretty great about myself, to be honest, and I think stepping up to help my mom fueled my belief that I could still be in charge of my life. To me, it was a logical choice.

Fortuitously, my decision wasn't subsequently undermined by what I learned while making the film. In fact, the opposite proved true. My decision to join a neighborhood gym the day after my diagnosis turned out to have been exactly the right thing to do. I learned of new research suggesting that vigorous exercise could help mitigate symptoms, and might even slow disease progression. I also learned more about how idiosyncratic Parkinson's is—that the disease varies markedly from person to person. An old saying in the Parkinson's world is, "If you've met one person with Parkinson's, you've met *one person* with Parkinson's."

Gaining more knowledge about the disease and interviewing leading scientists gave me hope that I could be one of the lucky ones. And while I'd seen what had happened to my dad during the disease's final stages, I also remembered how well he'd done for many years, and I chose to believe, armed with the latest research, personal history, and probably a dose of denial, that my own progression might be slow as well.

As paradoxical as it may seem, making *My Father, My Brother and Me* wound up reinforcing my reasons for becoming a caregiver. My life was focused on two things that felt mutually aligned, each activity affirming the other. I was learning more about the latest science and what my future might hold, but I was also learning more about our family story. My mom and I would sit by the fire, sipping scotch while she told me stories about my dad and their life together. I felt I had reason to be hopeful, and I sure as hell had reason to help my mom. I knew I couldn't do all that she had done for my dad, but I could be there. We could cheer for the same team.

I couldn't have fully articulated all of this at the time; I just remember feeling that I was doing exactly what I wanted, both at home and at work. It gave me a kind of steadiness. If staying in balance was what mattered most, as my doctor had wryly advised, maybe the intertwining of work and family was helping me discover how to achieve it.

My mom was proud that I was making the film, especially since it would be on PBS, the only channel she watched other than ESPN. And my brother Peter—a private person who'd never talked openly about having Parkinson's—surprised me by agreeing to participate in the documentary.

We filmed our interview on the back porch of the home we'd grown up in together. We talked about our shared experience, and then I asked him if he remembered what he'd said to me the day I called him to tell him I'd been diagnosed.

With a gentle smile, he said, "I don't, but I have a feeling you're about to remind me."

I did: "We're just going to have to fight this together."

I was getting ready to write the final script and begin editing the film when I decided there was still one other person I needed to film: my mom. I asked her if she'd be willing to do an interview. I wanted to get her perspective on my dad's Parkinson's—what she'd witnessed living alongside the man she loved.

She didn't hesitate. "Yes. I can do that."

We did the interview near the fireplace, my mom sitting in what had been my dad's favorite chair—the same one you can see my brothers and I crowded in and around on family Christmas cards dating back to the early 1950s. My mom and I began by talking about the first time she'd noticed that something might be amiss with my dad. She described his earliest symptoms with precision, including how my dad held one arm at an awkward angle when he walked—something I now found myself doing on occasion as well.

And then I asked her about what had been hardest for my dad about living with Parkinson's.

My father had been a gifted teacher, the kind who could hold a room with the elegance of his lectures and the warmth of his voice. He'd never lost his love for the spoken word, even decades removed from his days as a radio actor playing bit roles in *The Lone Ranger*, coupling a storyteller's skill with an educator's heart.

My mom paused, then replied, "It wasn't losing the ability to move. It was losing his voice."

I thought that might be her answer, though I'd never heard her say so before. But I knew it was true, and I knew she'd also identified the one thing I feared about Parkinson's, too.

✦

When the film was finished, we did a final pre-broadcast screening at *Frontline*'s headquarters in Boston. Sitting there watching, I experienced the kind of moment that had always marked my most satisfying work experiences. I'd had an idea, and I knew I had to make it happen. Now, several years later, it was real: a film about my family's saga with Parkinson's disease, and the political and scientific challenges that accompanied the search for a cure. I sat there watching as *Frontline's* signature opening animation and theme music resounded across the room. And then the documentary began, and I heard my voice narrating the opening line.

The film ends with my mom. I ask her how she feels about Parkinson's extending its reach to another generation of her family.

She looks at me and says, "Well, I hadn't thought it would happen. But it has happened. And when I see you go out for your walks and jogs, I just think how great that is and how hopeful I am. I refuse to think any other way."

7

YEAR 2:
A DARK RIVER

BY LATE JANUARY OF 2009, some fifteen months into my caregiving experience, I felt like things were starting to look up. Following my mom's lengthy hospitalization and rehab for the UTI and broken ankle, we settled back into life at her old home. And two good things had taken place during her convalescence: We'd met Eileen, who was now assisting us at home. And we'd watched the candidate my mom had championed be sworn in as the forty-fourth president of the United States.

Within a few months, my mom was once again able to use her walker and navigate the house on her own. We resumed attending Stanford basketball games, soon to be followed by trips to Sunken Diamond, home of the Stanford baseball team. And the fundamental rhythm of how she carried herself began to return as well. The nighttime disorientation she'd experienced at the hospital largely went away. Her smile still brightened the room. She still preferred men who were Democrats. She was still recognizably Adelaide.

By this point, I felt like I'd assembled an actual team. I now had Mele from 8:00 a.m. until 3:00 p.m., Monday through Friday, and Eileen from 4:00 p.m. until 6:30, with my brother, sister-in-law, or me checking in as well. Eileen's help meant I could work a longer day or get to the gym before taking over during the evening and on through the night. But even as those familiar patterns of behavior reassured me, something new was beginning to emerge.

My mom had always been confident of who she was, and her place in the world. But now it seemed she wasn't so sure about where she stood. Like most of us, she'd long had the habit of embellishing bits of her life story, but they were generally harmless fictions. Her "daily two-mile walk" was really only a one-mile stroll. Or during my dad's final years, she would recount how the two of them would talk at length about a current political campaign, even though I knew he was no longer able to do so. In time, I would come to understand that in their own way, with a nod or a smile, they probably *did* converse about politics. But at the time, I just thought she wanted to make sure people still saw my dad as someone who was fully engaged. It was hard to quarrel with that.

Regardless of my mom's propensity for exaggeration, I knew that her message was usually true at heart. But in the months following her hospital stay, I began to notice exaggerations of a different sort. She seemed to be embellishing the truth in order to ensure her own standing, to make sure others still saw her importance.

And to do so, her exaggerations often focused on what was wrong with people rather than what was right.

One day after work, I walked into the kitchen to greet my mom. She put down her *New York Times* and looked at me with grave concern.

"David, you won't believe what happened to me today." She went on to recount how Mele hadn't helped her in the bathroom. She'd been left there "for hours," before Mele finally returned.

I was incredulous.

"It was just awful," she continued in dramatic fashion. "I really didn't know if I would survive."

I knew she wanted sympathy, perhaps validation, but I was bewildered. I knew it couldn't be factually accurate, but I didn't want to be dismissive either.

"Are you sure it was really hours?" I said.

Yes, she was sure. Hours and hours.

"Well, I'm so sorry you had that experience," I said. "I'll talk to Mele if you want."

She nodded and went back to reading the newspaper.

✦

I was baffled by what she had said, but rather than spending more time trying to understand her experience, I worried instead about how Mele would react when I talked to her. The last thing I wanted was for Mele to think I doubted the quality of care she provided. What would happen if she were offended by Adelaide's accusation and quit? There's probably no greater source of dread for a family caregiver than imagining you might wind up doing it all yourself.

Perhaps my mom just wanted to tell the story and

bask in my sympathy. Perhaps she'd just forget all about it. After all, her remarkable ability to remember almost everything in her entire life, including which hotel she stayed at in Paris in 1936, had dulled over the past year. Still, I knew I needed to at least try to find out what had really happened, so I decided I'd talk to Mele but frame the story in a less dramatic way. I told Mele that Adelaide had said she'd been left in the bathroom for what felt to her like a really long time.

Mele broke into a wide grin and said, "David, when I went in to check on her after a few minutes, she'd nodded off. She was just sitting on the toilet, dozing. So I let her sit there for a few minutes, before waking her up."

I chose not to tell my mom what I'd found out, and she never brought it up again either. But in the months that followed, she would recount other examples of how she'd felt mistreated. And more significantly, Mele would tell me that Adelaide had been upset with her over some perceived failing. Mele always laughed it off, which is a wondrous quality in any caregiver. But it was worrisome, especially since my always conscientious sister-in-law Yoko, who came over each week to sit with Adelaide for an hour or two, would tell me that my mom was often unhappy with her over some alleged misdeed. Only Eileen, perhaps because she was the most imposing of the three, avoided being the target of criticism. But how do you fix a problem that isn't real except to the person who's complaining?

✦

I'm concerned that Adelaide will
continue to be negative, and that

Mele might decide to leave. The trick is, what do I say to Mom?

Should I be firm, or should I just ignore it, hoping she'll forget about it?

She usually does best when I just listen to her and then make some quiet observation. But there's definitely part of me that wants to get more hard-nosed, though that's probably not going to be effective.

—May 2009

✦

I decided my first approach would be to find any excuse to extoll Mele and Yoko's virtues, telling my mom how kind and attentive they were, and how lucky we were to have them in our lives. She would agree, but her litany of slights continued.

The more she was critical of others, the more I felt inclined to dispute her stories. I would lay out all the reasons why Mele and Yoko were great, and why her version of events wasn't true. I would present my best arguments, but I wasn't persuasive. It wasn't a winnable case, because all my evidence and testimonials no longer swayed a jury of one. Indeed, I was beginning to realize that the old adage "Everyone is entitled to their own opinions but not their own facts" wasn't really true. My mom wasn't expressing an opinion; she was expressing her own set of facts. And the only person who could set things straight was no longer fully present: Adelaide herself.

It wasn't that melodrama was entirely new to my mom. She'd always been capable of dramatic renditions of how she'd been wronged. But in the past, even if she initially stalked off in a huff, she always worked to make that crooked path straight. A family squabble? She'd pound out her frustrations on pie dough as she prepared to bake. Arguments with friends were rare, but readily resolved through cheering at a game or joining together to work on some community cause. She made things better by simply being better herself—by quickly turning her focus to good-deed doing.

But good deeds were harder to do now, which may have unconsciously fueled her own frustrations. Perhaps she felt slighted because she wasn't able to do more for herself or for others. The confusions and accusatory glares we'd experienced in the past year could be explained by raging infection from a UTI or pneumonia, but this was different. She wasn't in a fog, and she wasn't delusional. Rather, she seemed to be experiencing reality in a slightly different way.

It's often said that as we age, we become less constrained by our usual notions of what constitutes proper behavior. We become more direct and say whatever pops into our heads rather than being restrained by societal norms, as if our auto-edit function has been disabled. But I think my mom was experiencing something more complex than that. I don't think she was just delivering blunter assessments; I think she was also articulating her new reality.

For most of our lives, language helps us define what we think is true. But perhaps as we age, what we see as true also begins to redefine our language. In my mom's case, the world had become a less understandable place. If I go back to her story of being left alone in the bathroom, there are two ways to describe what happened. From our point of view, Adelaide hadn't been left alone in the bathroom for hours; she'd simply dozed off for a few minutes. But from her point of view, it must have felt something like this: She'd gone into the bathroom, and at some point she became alert to the fact that she'd been sitting there awhile, alone. She probably didn't realize she'd fallen asleep. She just knew she'd been left for what felt like a really long time. It wasn't "hours and hours," but her perception wasn't all fiction either. That it wasn't our version of reality doesn't make it less real. She wasn't so much making something up, as she was reporting her experience.

She was doing more than expressing her own set of facts. She was living them.

+

I wish I'd had this perspective at the time, but I didn't. I was just perplexed, and I was more likely to end up irritated than understanding. I didn't realize that she was still very much Adelaide; it's just that her reality was shifting to a different plane. But every so often, something would happen that would crack open a window into this brave new world.

It happened one afternoon when we were setting out to do something unremarkable. I'd wanted my mom to see some new photos of her great-grandchildren, so I opened up my laptop to show her. The screen remained dark for a long time. We kept staring, waiting for the photos to appear.

And then finally, my mom said, "It's like looking into a dark river and not being able to see the fish."

It was as if some novel neural connection had just been forged, and out poured a sentence that crystalized her perception, her set of facts—a truth that had never been articulated that way before, and never would be again.

+

One of caregiving's more difficult, but ultimately more rewarding, challenges is to recognize the truth that lies below what is said, to try to place yourself inside the other person's reality and then look outward onto what must be an unfamiliar and unsettling new terrain.

To focus on what someone is experiencing rather than what they are saying is no easy task—one I would fail at for a very long time. But there are moments when a new reality cracks open, when a dark river parts and we're offered a deep truth—one we would not have the privilege to see were we not in that person's presence and in their world.

8

FAMILY MATTERS

WHEN I WAS GROWING UP, our family dinner table conversations were usually taken up with politics, sports, and what each of us boys was up to in school. But once in a while, we also veered into religion. My mom, following the Schmitt tradition, was a devout Catholic, and my brothers and I all attended Sunday mass without fail. My dad was agnostic, staying home to watch football instead, and when I was a young teenager, I began to question our parents' diverging allegiances.

One evening during dinner, I mused aloud about why attendance at mass dropped during the summertime.

"Maybe it's like summer reruns on TV," I said. "People don't bother to go to church because they've already seen the show."

I could tell my dad thought this was funny, because he got up from the table, grinning, and walked to the kitchen sink, trying to keep from laughing out loud. My mom just sat there shaking her head, looking annoyed. My older brother, Peter, didn't say anything, but I'm pretty sure he was thinking something like: *I could never get away with saying that. But David gets away with anything.*

Throughout our lives, Peter has held the view that I had special status, that I could say and do stuff that he never could. This was not without justification. As the oldest son, he felt our folks were the toughest on him— more restrictive, more demanding—and he was right. Peter was a bright and diligent student, never taking a day off from school. I was bright, but more of a slacker—a trait that once prompted my high school French teacher to tell me, "Iverson, someday you're going to learn that the only way you can coast in life is downhill." Which is the only lesson I remember from high school French. And a pretty good one, at that.

It was true that I had more latitude on the home front, and I was capable of taking advantage of that leeway, especially in how I acted toward my mom. Once, after she got off the phone with a friend of hers, I mocked how she'd sounded, imitating her voice with the kind of offhand cruelty only a fifteen-year-old can muster. She put her face in her hands and then looked up with eyes that burned like embers and said:

"Someday you'll have a child, and I hope that child hurts you the way you just hurt me." And then she walked away.

I knew I'd screwed up, but I didn't realize how fully until my dad talked to me the next day. It's the only time I remember him taking me aside to deliver a message. He wasn't angry, just serious and a little sad. He told me that it wasn't right to treat my mom that way. It was never OK, he said, to hurt someone you loved, and who loved you.

Despite my adolescent behavior, my mom and I retained a special bond. Once, when I was a teenager and Peter was home from college, my mom got upset for reasons I can't remember. Eventually, she stalked off to her bedroom, closing the door firmly behind her. Peter and I sat there for a few minutes, and then I got up and walked back to the bedroom, tapped on the door, and entered. She was lying on the bed, staring at the ceiling. I reached out and she took my hands, pulling herself up, and together we walked back into the living room. I don't remember what was said, but everything was suddenly OK.

Later, after my mom had gone back to the bedroom, Peter turned to me and said, "I could never have done that."

+

Peter is four and a half years older than I am, Paul five years younger. As in most families, my brothers and I played different roles, both as kids growing up, and continuing on into adulthood. And I think the outlines of that family geometry were probably apparent early on, which is why the story about me looking up at my mom when I was three, and saying, "We sure like ourselves, don't we, Mom?" revealed a great deal about our personalities, and about a relationship that hit its defining stride right out of the gate.

Yes, as I got older we sometimes clashed. But I was also the one who could tease, cajole, or persuade our mom in a way no one else in our family could. And while it may have started when I was three and she was in her late thirties, it was just as true sixty years later. We were fundamentally at ease with one another, and that basic truth had everything to do with our lifelong relationship.

And I think that's why, who becomes the parental caregiver is pretty predictable. Picture you and your siblings. One of your parents needs care. You talk it over, but you already kind of know who it's going to be. That doesn't mean one family member is more virtuous, and the rest of the siblings are slackers. Other factors, especially gender and proximity, are part of the equation, too. But it's also about how personalities align.

My mom and I liked ourselves, which means we were both prone to self-satisfaction, sometimes to our mutual annoyance. But I also had the ability to coax, to smooth troubled waters and ease the way forward, and perhaps that was the most significant factor of all. I had the easiest relationship with the parent who needed help.

I think that's why when our mom needed care, who would do it wasn't a subject of lengthy conversation. There was no family meeting because it was already understood. Which is another reason why my choice to become a caregiver was a ten-second decision. It's also probably why my family greeted the decision with neither surprise nor applause. In fact, our mom's reaction was something close to nonchalance. Perhaps that's because, in a very real sense, this was an understanding forged long ago.

✦

My assuming caregiver duties may not have been the subject of family debate, but that didn't mean my brothers and I were guaranteed a tension-free future, especially since the choices you make in caregiving are often about money. In the coming years, my mom would need more care, and it would largely be up to me to decide how that would be financed. When I started out, our care costs were about $2,800 a month. But fifteen months later, that total had risen to $4,400, just by adding twenty hours of help each week. That amount exceeded the entirety of my mom's retirement income. Fortunately, the fifteen-hundred-square-foot home my parents purchased in Menlo Park in 1950, for $15,000 was now situated at the epicenter of the Bay Area's real estate boom. By the fall of 2007, when I moved in, the value of my parents' house had probably increased a hundredfold—equity that could help fund a lot of care costs, but that also had the potential to prompt family friction.

I thought about how we were going to finance my mom's care all the time. One concern was pragmatic—how to pay the bills—but I was also acutely aware that by spending nights and weekends with my mom, I was propping up the bottom line. If I hadn't, our monthly care costs would have more than doubled. The time I was putting in also lessened how much we had to borrow against the house, a house that someday my brothers and I would inherit. It feels weird to acknowledge that I occasionally thought about how my caregiving role might impact our collective financial well-being, but I did. On the other hand, I don't think that notion ever occurred to my brothers. That irked me sometimes because I wanted extra credit. But I got over it because I realized that sometimes there's great value in *not* talking about everything. Besides, I loved them, and they loved me.

We'd always shown up for each other during difficult times, and we understood our different life situations.

When I moved in with our mom, I was three years into my Parkinson's diagnosis, while Peter was fifteen years into a disease that was starting to take its toll. Paul, who is one of the most resilient people I've ever known, was dealing with his own health challenges. We understood our strengths and weaknesses, and mutual affection and shared history helped keep us on common ground.

My brothers, along with my sisters-in-law Kaaren and Yoko, also propped me up in other ways. They told me, with great regularity and sincerity, how much they appreciated what I was doing, and that improved my emotional bottom line—which counts for plenty. I also didn't have to worry about achieving family consensus when it came to every caregiving decision. By and large, the choices were mine, and if you're someone who likes taking charge, that's stress-reducing in and of itself.

All of this meant our family mostly stayed true to form. We were careful and courteous with each other. My brothers made sure I knew that they appreciated my efforts, and I knew I was doing something they couldn't. And if I was honest with myself, I had to admit that I wouldn't have wanted it any other way.

9

LYNN

LYNN AND I MET WHEN WE WERE KIDS, and started dating in high school. We were each other's first love, and like many such relationships, ours followed a familiar pattern—we broke up after we went off to college, yet retained a lifelong connection.

Our parents were casual friends, and though Lynn and I seldom saw each other in the decades following college, we stayed in touch and retained an easy ability to talk to each other. When we did get back together at the age of fifty, that easy rapport became one of our relationship's greatest strengths. We could talk about anything. But since I'd moved in with my mom, I was prone to letting my preoccupation with caregiving skew the nature of our conversations. Sometimes with comic results.

My becoming a caregiver happened to coincide with a renaissance in the fortunes of Stanford's beleaguered football team, and a few seasons later they were heading to the Rose Bowl for the first time in many years. Lynn and I were alums, and we were both excited to go. As the game approached, I began to think about how my mom had gone to see Stanford play in the 1952 Rose Bowl, only to see them get shellacked by Illinois, 52–7. The odds were better this time, and I'd started to wonder if I could get my mom back to Pasadena once more. The conversation that followed went like this:

Me: Don't you think it would be kind of cool if we took Adelaide to the Rose Bowl?

Lynn: I hope you two have a nice time.

Lynn is the most accommodating person on the planet. She respected my commitment to take care of my mom, and seemed quietly accepting of the choice I'd made. She went on with her busy life as a full-time elementary school teacher with three grown kids, and she would come down to Menlo Park one night a week to stay with her otherwise absent partner. But that doesn't mean she was enamored with our situation, and she would occasionally comment that it seemed like my mom was my first priority. I would offer fourteen reasons why that wasn't true, but spending seven nights a week at my mom's house didn't exactly reinforce my argument.

Which brings me to the central question I seemingly didn't want to address during my early years as a caregiver: What did I really want for Lynn and me?

Indeed, all I can find in my journal during this time are occasional questions that I didn't go on to answer.

✦

> What is it that I long for with
> Lynn? Do I want—really want—
> us to be together? Or have we
> waited too long?
>
> —June 2008

+

By that summer of 2008, Lynn and I had been together for nearly a decade. We were both approaching sixty, and while we were a committed couple, we were also committed singles. Before moving in with my mom, I had an apartment in San Francisco, while Lynn owned a house across the bay in Albany, just north of Berkeley. We'd never lived together. My decision to move in with my mom only increased our separation. So did I use my commitment to my mom as a way to avoid making a commitment to Lynn?

By contrast, during the time I stayed with my mom, I managed to be fully committed to achieving other goals. I made two documentary films for national broadcast on PBS. I hosted a radio show for San Francisco's NPR station, and I did both volunteer and professional work for the Michael J. Fox Foundation that mattered deeply to me. On a more personal level, I'd gotten myself in the best shape of my life, and was able to achieve more physically than I'd ever dreamed. Thanks to our caregivers, I could take time to get away and be with my daughter and her growing family back east. So I wasn't exactly neglecting other life priorities. But I had avoided answering a central question about the woman I loved: how to make that love fully real.

The cliché you always hear about caregiving is that you can't take care of someone else if you don't take care of yourself. Well, that's not true at all. You absolutely can. Caregivers do it all the time, and often sustain that ability for many years. There are logical reasons why that choice gets made—from feeling like no one else can do what you can, to knowing that finding backup help is usually a colossal pain, unaffordable, or both. I think I sometimes avoided getting the extra help I needed because, frankly, it was easier to give up time with Lynn than do what was necessary to make it happen.

The same applied to big life decisions. Caregiving is about as good an avoidance mechanism as you can come up with. It provides convenient cover. People would often tell me that I had a lot on my plate, and that was true. But what may have also been true was that, consciously or not, it was sometimes easier for me to keep it that way. Rather than answer tough questions about what the future held for Lynn and me, it was safer to focus on my caregiving responsibilities. Or when I did contemplate our options, to still factor my mom into the story.

+

I don't want to do this alone for too long. Could Lynn and I buy a small place in Palo Alto and have Adelaide move in with us?

—May 26, 2008

+

Like that was going to happen. Lynn is the most generously inclined person I know, yet my even suggesting such a notion would have prompted—even in Lynn—wide-eyed astonishment. But saying that our relationship was put on hold primarily because of caregiving's demands is also too easy. In fact, caregiving put into sharper focus an aspect of my personality that impacted both my ability to be a caregiver and to nourish a caring relationship with Lynn: my tendency to think I'm always right.

When Lynn came down to Menlo Park on Saturday night, we'd often have long talks about what was going on in our lives: our work, our adult children, and what I felt compelled to do for my mom. One Saturday night, I was particularly intent on making a certain point about some topic I've long since forgotten.

Within seconds, Lynn said, "Yeah, that's true. You're right."

To which I responded, honest to God, "But wait, I'm not done being right!"

Fortunately, we both burst out laughing.

My mom would have rolled her eyes at that conversation.

I once overheard her say to Eileen, "David just thinks he's right about everything, even though he isn't. But we'll just let him think that way."

I could just as easily have been overheard saying the same thing about her. Even as my mom became more diminished, she was still capable of holding forth from center stage, with pronouncements I didn't always greet too charitably.

One morning, my mom told me she'd been a Rhodes Scholar, another time that she'd gone to law school. I knew she was starting to slip cognitively, but I still couldn't let go of my desire to set the record straight. I would gently explain to her why she was wrong, and tell her what I thought was right. After a while, I would grow frustrated and either just change the subject, or leave the room. Sometimes my exasperation would manifest in sudden bursts of anger. I remember once bumping into my mom's walker and kicking it out of the way while barking, "Get the goddamn walker out of the way!" and then stomping away.

I would get angry because I could no longer make my mom understand how right I was. It took me an absurdly long time to appreciate that if at age ninety-seven, my mom believed she'd gone to law school, why cling to a purely objective view of truth? After all, she easily could have gone to law school, and probably should have. My being right was of precious little import, and my frequent failure to recognize that truth affected other relationships in my life—most particularly with Lynn.

In time, being a caregiver helped me begin to realize that an intimate relationship—which is what caregiving is—depends in no small measure on the ability to pay attention—to listen and adapt accordingly. Acceptance and adaptability are at the heart of what loving care requires, to see how someone is changing, and then be ready to shift and improvise as necessary rather than stay committed to whatever strategy you'd recently adopted— like, maybe yesterday.

Being a good caregiver is a little like being a jazz musician—always adapting, tuned to every call, and nimble in each response. And the core values true caregiving requires are central to all healthy human interaction: kindness, honesty, selflessness, and generosity. And it's why, over the long haul—in my case, the *really* long haul—caregiving offered me an opportunity to get marginally better at manifesting those attributes. Caring for my mom put my particular Achilles heel—being Mr. Right—squarely in the crosshairs. Like a heat-seeking missile, caregiving seeks out your flash points and pierces your defenses. It continually exposes your vulnerabilities, and therein is the silver lining. If there are aspects of your personality that need adjustment, I can think of no better self-improvement course than caregiving.

That character-building opportunity happens, in part, because, unlike most relationships, the caregiving experience offers plenty of built-in second-chance opportunities. As the late Harvard chaplain Peter Gomes once observed, there are few things more inspiring than being granted another morning. You screwed up part of yesterday, Gomes notes, and you'll probably screw up part of today. But we're granted another morning, and that's enough.

Thankfully, that means those of us who stumble along as caregivers get plenty of do-overs. What's just as crucial to remember is that the person we're caring for gets another morning, too. Her day may not start out as you had hoped, but if you can wake up ready to be present and responsive to *that* person, not the person she was yesterday or the person you long for her to be, then you're making progress.

And to my great good fortune, Lynn gave me plenty of do-overs, too.

✦

In Lin-Manuel Miranda's *Hamilton*, Aaron Burr gives Alexander Hamilton some shrewd advice. Miranda's Hamilton thought he was always right, and would relentlessly tell people why.

Burr offers his rival this counsel: "Talk less. Smile more."

Holding back isn't easy when you feel you're right, especially if you're tired, especially if you're frustrated. But holding back is crucial if what you're about to say would diminish the person in front of you. To state what should have been obvious to me, but often wasn't: What matters most when we're engaged in an intense conversation with someone we love—be it parent or partner—isn't the summation of our talking points. It's where our words will lead us. Will they take us toward kindness and generosity? Will our words strengthen and fortify this relationship we cherish? Or are we too busy being right?

Talk less. Listen more. Be kind. I often try to remind myself of something I learned in journalism but was exponentially reinforced through caregiving: "All that needs to be said is all that needs to be said."

And if you don't believe this yet, just wait. You'll see.

I'm right about this.

10

NIGHT
IN THE GARDEN OF SORROW

IT WAS OFTEN AROUND 1:00 A.M. when the bell would ring. My mom was heading for the bathroom, and that meant I was headed there, too. My bedroom was just ten feet from my mom's, and when she headed for the bathroom, I would usually hear the thump of her walker leaving the bedroom carpet and landing on the hallway's hardwood floor. But on occasion, I'd miss that telltale thud. Since it wasn't safe for her to go to the bathroom on her own, my nephew Jens and I installed a hallway bell with a button by her bedside that she could ring when she got up at night. And if it rang before 2:00 a.m., that meant I was likely in for a three-bell night.

I would stumble into the bathroom and whip on a pair of gloves—something I could now do quickly, even when half asleep. When my friends would ask me about helping my mom, the euphemistic phrase, "helping in the bathroom," would occasionally come up. A certain look would come over my male friend's faces in particular, but an experience that once seemed unimaginable becomes pretty ordinary over time. And that wasn't just true for me; it was true for my mom, too. When it was necessary to collect a urine sample to test for a UTI, I eventually became adept at performing what's known as a "clean catch," and I remember my mom and I both laughing the first time we shared that experience. It gave the phrase "being in it together" a whole new meaning.

"Helping in the bathroom" actually turns out to be pretty easy. You wipe, you flush, and you're finished. It's not what happens when you head for the bathroom that's problematic; it's what happens when you head back to bed.

I'd always been a good sleeper, only waking a time or two a night, and almost always able to get back to sleep readily. But now it wasn't my own biological clock that would awaken me; it was someone else's. It's a bit like going to bed at night without setting your alarm but knowing that it was going to go off at random intervals anyway. And once the bell rang the first time, I knew it would likely ring again.

Sometimes I felt like I was rewinding the clock to when I'd been a parent of an infant, and a good night's sleep felt like a distant dream. But now I was thirty years older, and being sleep-deprived impacted the rest of my life that much more. We all know that sleep is a precious commodity, but caregiving requires you to experience the biology of that truth in a brand-new way. Of all the challenges one confronts in caregiving, for me none was more unforgiving than lack of sleep and its consequences.

I became more short-tempered. Sometimes the targets were inconsequential, like kicking my mom's walker out of the way. But I was also more prone to snapping at my mom or letting Lynn bear the brunt of my unhappiness.

✦

> I'm definitely feeling and acting
> more negative, especially around
> Lynn. Perhaps because she
> doesn't chastise me for it.... It's
> like I'm making the point that my
> life is tough—I'm going to show
> her how challenging my life is.
>
> —May 4, 2008

✦

Getting a good night's sleep may be an obvious priority, but acknowledging its importance isn't the same as devising a specific plan to achieve it, especially if you're short on the clarity and focus you need to create one. Even something as seemingly straightforward as getting a single night off suddenly seems daunting. After all, I'm surviving, I found myself saying, shouldn't I stick it out as long as I can?

But here's a caregiving truth I believe in: All family caregivers need more help then they think they do. And all caregivers come to that realization later then they should.

Even if you're fortunate enough to have the resources I did, you can't help but wonder if those resources will be sufficient. You tell yourself you can manage. We all think we can manage.

Take my friend Margaret. Margaret's husband has advanced dementia, and she cares for him at home. She has help, but she still provides a tremendous amount of personal care. Plus, she handles all the household responsibilities and manages her own business. Margaret's challenges were greater than mine, and it had taken a toll. One day, she started having shooting pains down her arm. She thought she might be having a heart attack, but rather than call 911, she felt she first had to make dinner for her husband and their helper. Finally, she drove herself to the hospital. They determined her heart was fine, but suspected an anxiety attack. To make sure, they kept her overnight for observation. And what happened next? Margaret slept. She later told me that it was the most restful night she'd had in a long time. It might not be the best strategy for getting a night off, but it worked.

In my case, I had two nighttime challenges to solve: three-bell nights, and covering nights when I was out of town. So far, I had just pieced together various one-off solutions for the latter circumstance. But a better answer was right in front of me. I wasn't the only one who had a problem with sleep. Eileen was still spending weeknights on the floor at her parents' apartment, and it occurred to me that I could invite her to stay in my mom's extra bedroom instead. I didn't want to ask her to take over night duty on an ongoing basis, both for cost reasons and because she had to get up at 5:00 a.m. to go to her day job. But if she was willing to do night duty when I was away on business, then at least I'd have a built-in arrangement for overnight care. So I asked Eileen if she'd like to move in, plus make some extra money when I was away. She readily agreed. This was a solution worth a celebration. Or better still, worth a good night's sleep.

I now had a plan to handle nights when I was away for work, but it was the three-bell nights that were the real killers. That was especially true on the weekend, when I had solo duty from Friday evening until Monday morning. Getting sufficient sleep was central to managing those long weekend stretches. And there was an added factor: Lynn had been faithfully coming down from her home north of Berkeley on Saturday nights for a year and a half. Sometimes we'd take my mom out to dinner, or go to a Stanford game. The two of us would get in a short walk and have Sunday morning breakfast before Lynn would make her hour drive back home. But three-bell nights weren't exactly conducive to restful, let alone romantic, evenings, and Lynn finally suggested what should have been obvious: that I come up to her house one night a week instead. After all, it would be good for both of us. But since Eileen went home to see her family on the weekends, I would need to cast about for additional help. And fittingly, my mom indirectly helped provide the solution.

My mom was a loyal and committed friend. One of my favorite stories about her enduring friendships involved her longstanding treks to the Stanford campus neighborhoods where many of her dearest friends from the Stanford Village days still lived. On one of those trips a few years before I moved in, she'd apparently wowed her young cab driver with her intimate knowledge of the campus, prompting him to say, "You sure know your way around this place. Did you know Leland Stanford?"

My mom didn't quite go all the way back to the days of Stanford's nineteenth-century founder, but she was committed to standing by her oldest friends. One of them was a nearly blind woman named Sally. My mom had gone to her home to read to her each week, without fail.

I'd met Sally's caregiver a few times over the years—a lovely woman named Sinai Latu. Sally had passed away recently, so I called Sinai to see if she'd be willing to spend one night a week at my mom's. She'd already secured another position, but she said she'd make it work. Adelaide had made a difference in her life.

"Adelaide would come every week, and she would read and talk with Sally for two or three hours at a time," Sinai said. "She'd always thought about what Sally was interested in, bringing newspaper articles or a new book. Those visits were sometimes the only break I'd get. If you need help, then I'll be there."

✦

I now had two key components of a sustainable caregiver strategy: a reliable, skilled, and compassionate caregiving team, and a day off for myself each week. I should have felt great. But I didn't. Even after Sinai took over Saturday nights, I still found myself teetering on that cliff's edge where weariness topples into aggravation. I was getting respite, but I wasn't feeling recharged. On my best days, I might even have been on my way to becoming a better person, but that didn't mean the caregiving fundamentals had changed. My life was still largely governed by meeting someone else's needs. It was the organizing principle of my day. And one night, nearly two years after I'd moved in, everything came unglued—including me.

My mom's house had always been the location for larger family gatherings. But in recent years, my dad's youngest sister, Alice, had taken over most of those hosting duties. On this particular night, Alice was having my mom and me and the rest of the family over for dinner. And from the moment my mom's walker hit Alice's living room floor with an aggravated thump, I had the sense that we were all in for it. She wasn't happy, snapping at my sister-in-law Yoko when she offered her an hors d'oeuvre, complaining about where she was sitting, and responding crossly when one of us tried to respond to her grievances. Over the next hour, I found myself getting more and more irritated. Finally, I stepped over to her and said—exactly as I would have to a four-year old—"If you can't act better, we're going home."

A few minutes later, we headed for the dinner table. I didn't know you could stalk across the floor while using a walker, but my mom did. Alice asked her where she wanted to sit, and my mom snapped at her again. That did it.

"That's it," I said. "We're going home."

I steered her out of the room, out the doorway, and into the car. We drove home in silence.

I'd seen my mom put on performances like this before, and she'd sometimes aim her harshest words at those who were trying the hardest to be accommodating. It had happened when I'd first tried using substitute caregivers, as well as with Yoko and Mele. And I knew it would likely happen again.

When we arrived back at the house, I ushered her

into her bedroom with hands as comforting as steel. She stood next to her bed for a moment, gripping her walker, and then just collapsed onto the bedspread.

"I hate myself," she wailed.

And here's the thing: I didn't say a word. I didn't feel anything other than a cold sense of satisfaction.

I was acting like a self-righteous parent who'd appropriately reprimanded a bratty but now repentant child. But as I look back, I don't think I fully took in what my mom was saying. I think when she said she hated herself, she meant exactly that. She hated who she was becoming—hated the sense that she was increasingly trapped in a world where she could no longer be who she'd always been, including the person who'd always hosted family occasions.

My mom's wail was from the heart, but sometimes I felt like my own had turned cold.

✦

It wasn't until the next morning that I realized it wasn't just my mom who was becoming less becoming. I was, too, and I struggled with what I ought to do next. Should I apologize to my mom? And if so, what exactly should I apologize for? I felt my anger had been justified. My mom had behaved badly, and she was becoming increasingly difficult with people who were trying their best to help. It wasn't just how she'd treated my Aunt Alice; her criticisms of my sister-in-law Yoko and our daytime caregiver, Mele, had also continued to increase. And I was annoyed that she didn't seem to appreciate my efforts either, which wasn't exactly motivating my desire to continue. For the first time, but far from the last, I was facing the challenge most caregivers eventually confront: the moment when you just don't know if you want to do this anymore.

Early on in my caregiving experience, I'd often talked about all that I was learning while caring for my mom. But now I found myself talking more about how weary I was becoming. I'd come to realize that, for me at least, caring for a needy parent was fundamentally different than caring for a child. I could have stayed up through the night, long night after long night, to care for Laura, the daughter I love. The pain and worry would have been greater, but that pain would also have added meaning to the moment. I wouldn't be questioning why I was there. Indeed, I wouldn't want to be anyplace else. And perhaps more than anything, I wouldn't feel alone because I would be accompanied by unconditional love. But my love for my mom was becoming more conditional. I loved her, but I also wanted more sleep and more space—more life, really. Frustration was overtaking fulfillment. I was wearing out, and I wasn't sure how long I could continue.

But the morning after our blowup, I also felt regret—regret that I'd treated my almost hundred-year old mom like a four-year old. I told her I was sorry that I'd gotten angry, and that we'd both just have to keep doing the best we could. I probably also said something like, "I'm not going anywhere, and apparently you aren't either." I wasn't angry anymore. I just felt stuck.

That's what I was feeling one Sunday evening a few weeks later, when it was time to head for church. For decades, my mom had been part of Stanford's Catholic community, attending Sunday evening mass at the

Stanford Memorial Church. And even though I usually got something out of going, I increasingly found it to be one more thing I'd rather not do.

But off we went. And as the service progressed, I found myself being soothed by the twin comforts of a familiar service and the perpetually friendly Stanford Catholic community. They all loved my mom, who was always at her best at church, and basked in being beheld as such a marvel.

Today's gospel and homily were about Christ's lonely night in the garden at Gethsemane. And as Father Carl spoke, I began to pay more attention. He talked about how Christ wanted his suffering to end, and perhaps even more, how he wanted to be relieved of his profound sense of being alone and forsaken. It's like that for us, too, he said. Sometimes we turn to prayer, asking God to take away our suffering, but that's not really how prayer works. Rather, he argued, the purpose of prayer is to ask for the strength we need to face whatever is set before us. And we find that strength more readily when we place ourselves in the company of others.

As I wheeled my mom out of church into the early evening cold, I'm sure I wasn't alone in thinking about how I might apply Father Carl's homily to my own situation. To be sure, living with my mom was hardly the stuff of Gethsemane. It was becoming more challenging, yet I knew what I was experiencing was not remotely akin to true suffering. But whether we find ourselves in a state of deep sorrow, or are merely exhausted, we all wind up in the garden at some point, brought low by our challenges or our choices—by the pain life inevitably inflicts on us, or the pain we inevitably inflict on ourselves.

In the days ahead, I began to feel that as much as I wanted to wish my trials away, running from them wasn't going to solve the problem. Sure, I could move out and try to cobble together replacement care. But how would I really feel about that? Empty, I thought. It wasn't the right time to move out and move on. Which is not to say there aren't times when we must walk away—when we must fundamentally change our caregiving circumstance. But for reasons I couldn't articulate at the time, I wasn't ready to do that. I wasn't done. And my mom wasn't done either.

As I thought about it more, I realized that the problem wasn't that I was weary of caring for someone else; it was that the caring no longer felt fulfilling. Instead, I just felt alone. That thought took me back to what I'd felt that Sunday afternoon at Memorial Church, sitting in that beautiful and reflective space. I remembered that, at least for a moment, I'd felt accompanied and comforted, both by the message of the service and by the reassuring embrace of that community. I needed that because...well, we all need that.

And that allowed me to realize something else: despite my cranky self-righteousness, I was most likely still embraceable. I had let the cross-currents of caregiving bring me low, giving in to anger and frustration with more frequency than I wanted to admit. Maybe that was because I was doing something hard. I wouldn't feel like crap, I realized, if I didn't care. And sure, aspects of caring for my mom sucked. But that's how life is sometimes. Love and sorrow are intertwined. Why would I ever think otherwise?

I was still in the garden, but I didn't have to be alone.

11

HOME

MY MOM HAD ALWAYS PROVIDED a welcoming presence in our neighborhood, whether it was bringing over a plate of pastries for a new family, or making sure everyone on the block was registered to vote. She made people feel like they knew they were home. And there was something about the house itself that also brought comfort. For my brothers and me and our children, I think it had to do with the fact that it never changed.

A dozen years after they moved in, my parents added a few new pieces of furniture in what for them was a colossal spending spree, and then the house had ever so gently frozen in time. And now the house extended its welcome to our newest arrivals, Mele, Eileen, and Sinai. It seemed to foster a sense of place and purpose for each of them. They would often tell me how much they just liked being there—liked doing this work in a place that felt like home. They knew they were valued, and they valued that sense of belonging in return.

Even when one of them had to move on, our common bond continued. When Mele eventually decided she had to leave us because working two jobs was too much to manage alongside her growing family, she continued to visit. She'd pop in to show off her new baby, or bring her kids over on Halloween, one of my mom's favorite days. It wasn't easy to replace someone so irrepressibly cheerful, but Eileen decided to quit her day job so that she could be with Adelaide through the day, and I was able to find another helper through the agency I'd used before to cover Eileen's original hours.

Roanet Morales was a lively young woman originally from Nicaragua, who also had another full-time job, working the night shift at Stanford Hospital. But she could give us fifteen to twenty hours a week. And that, plus having Eileen all day during the week, and Sinai on Saturday night, left me feeling pretty fortunate.

Roanet was also a talented artist who would eventually create a giant mural for us, consisting of images from Adelaide's life: my dad walking on the beach with two of their grandchildren; the Stanford campus; a baseball glove; my mom's favorite coffee mug; and a mockup of *The New York Times*, with the headline, "Vote Democratic."

But best of all, Roanet had spark. She took my mom places: to nearby flower gardens; to see a local pumpkin festival in the fall; and to the beach, one of my mom's favorite destinations. When a new film of mine premiered at a Bay Area film festival a few years later, it was Roanet who made sure Adelaide was in the front row.

Roanet left us after a few years, too, when working

two jobs became too much. But like Mele, she stayed in touch, providing crucial updates on who she was dating, which Adelaide always relished. Roanet and Mele and I remain in contact to this day. Mele texts me every holiday, and Roanet continued to provide boyfriend updates to Eileen and me right up until she got married.

Eileen and Sinai would stay alongside me for the length of our shared caregiving journey. Some of that was just good fortune, but it was also more than that. For starters, we genuinely liked each other. We knew enough to cultivate mutual caring and do what was needed to sustain it. We would stay up late and talk. We'd ask after each other's families. And in time, we knew each other's stories.

I learned about how Sinai had come to this country alone, to better support her extended family back in Tonga. In addition to her caregiving jobs, I learned she made extra money by crafting beautiful baskets and sending the proceeds to Tonga to support her parents and a brother in need.

I learned about Eileen's childhood in Fiji. I learned about her first love; her extended family, where everyone seemed to be either an aunt or a cousin; and how she contended with family disapproval, on both sides, when she married a Muslim man.

Eileen and Sinai were both deeply religious. Eileen had converted to Islam, and Sinai was Christian. Faith was integral to their chosen profession.

As Sinai once said to me: "God put me here for a reason. When I walk through these doors, I feel like I belong, like part of the family."

Because she now took care of my mom on Sunday morning, Sinai wasn't able to attend her regular church service. When I asked her about that, she didn't seem particularly bothered.

"Don't worry about it," she'd always say. "I'm fine."

Several years would go by before I got enough extra help so that she could attend church once more, and she was radiant in her happiness; she had missed church terribly. But what I also came to understand was that she hadn't pretended to be OK just for my benefit; she really was.

Sinai put it like this: "My friends at church used to call and say that it was too bad that I couldn't go. But I told them, God chose Adelaide first."

In her view, she was in God's company when she attended to Adelaide, every bit as much as when she attended church. Taking care of Adelaide was the obvious choice because that's what allowed her to be true to the path she wished to follow.

Eileen had a big personality that lit up a room. We talked easily and often. Sometimes she'd join me for a late dinner after Adelaide was in bed, and we'd talk for hours. Sitting around that old kitchen table felt like a new variation on our family dinnertime conversations. Only, this time I was hearing about what Eileen's children were doing in school. It wasn't easy for her, being away from her kids during the week, but I knew she valued being able to talk about her family in the comfort of Adelaide's kitchen. I valued it, too.

Sinai's presence was softer but no less impactful. She'd arrive every Saturday evening with flowers because she knew Adelaide loved them. She'd sit with Adelaide and watch her beloved Stanford Cardinal on TV. And while I had a checkered record of getting my mom to Sunday evening mass, when Sinai was there, she got her to church on time and without fail.

Years later, I asked her what qualities she thought mattered most in her profession.

"I try to look at my patients the same way I'd look at my mom or grandmother," she said. "I try to care for them in the same way. And I try to only talk to them with my heart."

There was another reason our relationship grew stronger over time. They knew how much they mattered to me, and I knew how much Adelaide and I mattered to them. And while that deepening bond was defined by affection and appreciation, it was also defined by professional regard. I valued what they did—in part, because I had learned how freaking hard this work was—and I paid them accordingly. Watching them care for my mom reinforced what I was coming to understand—that caregiving can only be fully given when your heart is inclined toward kindness, kindness made real in its specificity: the way you help someone get dressed, the way you listen when the person you're caring for is cranky, the way you're willing to walk back into the room no matter what.

It sounds like an impossibly tall order, but that's exactly why professional caregivers should be valued far more than they are.

Eileen, Mele, Sinai, and Roanet all had the capacity to focus on what my mom needed, and to attend to those needs with good cheer at least 90 percent of the time. My own scorecard was far more inconsistent. I was committed to staying the course, but it was difficult for me not to have expectations—to accept that there really was an element of sailing into the unknown, and that unpredictable winds would keep redirecting whatever well-plotted chart I'd created. I found it endlessly challenging to both adapt to that world and to accept the limitations of my place in it. But Eileen and Sinai understood that I was trying my best, and they admired my attempts, even as I would often fall short. And it mattered to me, comforted me, and sustained me to know they understood. And in so doing, they also expanded my understanding of what family can actually mean.

Take what happened a few years later, when Eileen told me that it was time for my mom to use a hospital bed. I knew she was right, but I almost immediately began dreading having to move my mom's queen bed out of her bedroom. But late one night, a few days later, the doorbell rang. It was Eileen's eighteen-year-old son and three of his Pacific Islander pals, who all looked big enough to be starting linemen for the Stanford football team. Eileen had asked them to help move the furniture, so they'd driven the seventy miles from Eileen's home to Menlo Park at 11:00 p.m. to do just that.

When I asked Eileen later, how she'd cajoled four teenagers into lending a helping hand, she said, "Because you and Adelaide are family, and I'm the mom."

✦

The meaning of home and family, career and care-giving, began to change for me during those years. Each became more interdependent with the other, more intertwined. Caring for my mom alongside Eileen and Sinai deepened my understanding of not only what caring can mean, but career, too, including what it means to be a journalist. I don't think it's a coincidence that the two most satisfying film projects of my career took place while I was a caregiver: my *Frontline* film on Parkinson's, and another documentary which would be the last film I would make for PBS.

When I was working on the *Frontline* project, I'd heard about a group called Dance for PD, a New-York-City-based dance program for people with Parkinson's, led by members of the renowned Mark Morris Dance Group. The first time I walked into their Brooklyn studio, I saw a remarkable sight: people with Parkinson's joined by spouses, caregivers, and two of the best modern dancers in the world, David Leventhal and John Heginbotham, all dancing together. I did a short piece about the program for the *PBS NewsHour*, but when I learned they were joining forces to put on a first-of-a-kind dance performance in New York City, I knew I wanted to create a feature documentary, following them from first rehearsal to final performance.

Because I had a limited budget and a limited number of nights I could be away from home, I'd sometimes fly to New York on a red-eye, film all day, and then fly back to the West Coast that same evening. But I was always invigorated by what I witnessed: a group of people from different backgrounds, with different abilities and different life stories, forging an extraordinary bond. They showed me what happens when people stand together, then step out onto a new stage. In a time when the idea of American community was becoming an oxymoron, they were a reminder of what dedication, sacrifice, and shared humanity can create. As one of the dancers with Parkinson's says in the film, "When the music starts, there are no patients. There are only dancers."

The film was called *Capturing Grace,* and making it reminded me of an old journalistic truth: that our primary job is to pay attention, to watch for—and listen to—those who have a story to tell.

Telling their story was the greatest privilege of my filmmaking career, and it was also a reminder to adhere to the same guiding purpose at home—to listen to my mom's story and respond to the truth at its core.

+

That same intertwining of work, home, and caregiving also deepened my perspective on stories I'd sometimes covered on the radio, like immigration. Until I became a caregiver, I hadn't had good friends who'd had to work two jobs or sleep on the floor in order to make ends meet. I hadn't seen the skill and compassion it takes to attend to someone else's most basic needs, and to do so with tenderness and ease. And I hadn't understood—at least, not in such an intimate way—the additional challenges you sometimes face if your name is Taufa, Morales, Khan, or Latu. When your skin is brown and English is your second or third language. Their lives told a different story than the talk shows I sometimes moderated on topics like whether all immigrants should possess specialized, technological skills before being allowed into this country.

In a nation where there will soon be nearly eighty million people over the age of sixty-five, just who do we think will provide care for those in need? And how do we think those skills should be valued?

Eileen and Sinai, along with Mele and Roanet, enhanced my life every bit as much as they did my mom's. It surprised me how enriching and important those relationships quickly became. And when unexpected kindness enters your life at a time when you need it most, it washes over your very being, releasing a wave of gratitude that can carry you through the great swirls of uncertainty that will so often surround you. You begin to realize that you are not entirely alone—not when someone offers the simple but extraordinary act of just being there when it's needed most.

My mom and I were living under the same roof once more, but it was really Sinai and Eileen who turned that old house back into a home. A home that now included three remarkable women rather than just one.

II

STILL HERE

12

GOING THE DISTANCE

IN THE SPRING OF MY MOM'S HUNDREDTH YEAR, we began planning a celebration. We made up Team Adelaide T-shirts for the occasion, with the number one hundred on the back. My mom was still sharp enough to relish the prospects. She went through her old address book and figured out who to invite. Her grandchildren and great-grandchildren flew in from as far away as the Netherlands. Her nieces and nephews came from afar. Even the sons and daughters of some of her late friends were in attendance.

It was a grand gathering, held on the back patio of the red tile roofed Stanford Golf Course restaurant, nestled under the California live oaks and framed against the surrounding foothills. My mom's four grandchildren—my daughter, Laura, and her cousins Ayuko, Erika, and Jens—all spoke lovingly of their grandmother, whose forceful presence and tender affections had always provided a grounding force in their lives. Peter, Paul, and I spoke, and Peter and his son Jens came up with an Adelaide trivia contest. We ate, drank, and told stories, and we read from the many congratulatory letters she'd received, including notes from California Governor Jerry Brown, and her great favorite, President Barack Obama.

Not surprisingly, the letters she delighted in most were from the Stanford basketball, football, and baseball coaches. The baseball coach recalled the time Adelaide had thrown out the first pitch five years earlier, and noted that he could still use an extra arm in the bullpen. And the basketball coach remembered that Adelaide couldn't abide missed free throws, and promised they were working hard on correcting that problem.

When we were all done with the festivities, had sung happy birthday and delivered our last toast, my mom did something that was pure Adelaide. As we gave her one last salute, she started to stand—something she hadn't been able to do without assistance for some time. Eileen and Sinai were sitting nearby, ready to help, but they must have known that Adelaide wanted to stand up solo and be counted.

She struggled to her feet and gave a short wave. She was still here. And so were we.

+

A few months later, I flew to New York to attend a meeting of the Michael J. Fox Foundation's Patient Council. Being on the Patient Council allowed me to stay up on the latest Parkinson's research, and during the meeting, Dr. Brian Fiske, one of the foundation's neuroscientists, gave a presentation that included an intriguing analogy that stuck with me. He said that trying to solve the riddle of Parkinson's disease was like piecing together a gigantic multi-billion-piece jigsaw puzzle, except this puzzle didn't include a box with a cover picture to guide you—nor were there any pieces with corners or straight edges. In that circumstance, he said, it's sometimes hard to know where to start, or when you're making progress.

Brian's analogy was apt for Parkinson's researchers. But in a more mundane sense, it also applied to the challenge caregivers confront: there's no picture on the caregiving puzzle box, and no corner pieces to guide you, so it's equally hard to know where to start and whether you're making progress.

I sometimes felt like caregiving was a maze with a million variations. Yet there was also a relentless sameness to each piece of the challenge. As I tried to find my way forward, I'd often feel like I'd already tried a particular option—probably because I had. And when I thought I'd finally found the right pieces, they usually didn't fit after all, and that often left me feeling like I wanted to knock the whole damn puzzle to the floor.

That's what happened not long after I returned from New York. I can't remember why, but I became furious with my mom. I just recall lecturing her about something, which prompted a few tears, which only infuriated me further.

"Just go ahead and cry," I shouted, and then stomped out of the room and into the garage, slamming the door behind me.

I remember just standing there, staring at the walls and hearing the rain falling on the roof. And then after a moment, all the anger drained out of me. I walked back into the kitchen and slumped down in the chair next to my mom and burst into tears, sobbing.

After a while, my mom whispered, "Don't cry, David. Don't cry."

✦

One of the best pieces of caregiving advice I ever received was simply, "Get used to it," because caregiving isn't a linear experience. You struggle, you find your way though, and then you struggle all over again, sometimes losing it altogether in the process.

✦

> I feel like I'm reaching an end
> point—that not only have I
> prevailed upon myself enough,
> I've prevailed on others,
> especially Lynn, for too long.
> So by mid-September, I need to
> either have someone else take
> over, or have Adelaide in a home.
> I have to make this happen.
>
> —July 2013

✦

But I didn't make it happen, just as I hadn't when I'd flirted with bailing out a few years before. What stopped me was always the same realization—a sense that I wasn't done. I still felt compelled to stay, and so I did.

The phrase "the loneliness of the long-distance runner" usually refers to running's solitary nature and the sense of escape it can bring. So it's probably not coincidental that I took up that activity around this time. To an extent, I was using one solo journey to escape another, while at the same time, engaging in the kind of vigorous exercise I knew was central to my ability to live well with Parkinson's. But it led to an outcome I never would have imagined—that while in my sixties and living with my mom, I'd run in four consecutive New York City Marathons to raise money for the Michael J. Fox Foundation.

Running taught me how much can be gained—perhaps especially later in life—when you accomplish something you never thought you could. You learn that you only get to the other side by pushing through obstacles that once seemed insurmountable. And in so doing, your sense of what gives life meaning begins to shift, revealing new routes and new destinations.

My closest friend, Gary, decided he wanted to run with me in my second New York City Marathon, and he would drive from his home in Oakland to Menlo Park so that we could go for training runs together. We'd loop around the Stanford campus, where we'd met as students forty-five years before—up and down Palm Drive, through the eucalyptus groves, around the Quad, and circling through the campus neighborhoods where my mom's old friends had once lived. I didn't think about anything when I was running—no problem solving, no musing, no nothing. I loved the mindlessness of it, coupled with its intense physicality. All that mattered was the next step.

As an older runner, I learned that I needed to be particularly mindful of what my body was telling me, and adjust my training regimen accordingly. And that experience helped me realize that I needed to apply the same approach to caregiving. I needed to develop a caregiving training regimen, too. So I asked Sinai if she could stay with my mom two nights a week rather than one, and that one-night extension made a huge difference, not just in the rest it provided, but in the anticipation it induced. I would count the hours until Sinai arrived; the prospect of going up to Lynn's for the weekend was that enticing. I felt like a teenager with a touch of Saturday night fever. When she arrived, I would literally jog across the front yard, hop in my car, and head off to what felt like a first date. And I tried my best to just relish that feeling, even though I knew it wouldn't last once I returned to Menlo Park.

✦

To my great surprise, running in my second marathon was harder than the first, even though Gary and I were running side by side. For me, the last seven miles were excruciating. Gary, on the other hand, was feeling great. He was happy and chatty. It drove me crazy.

Finally, somewhere around mile twenty-three, I turned to him and said, "Gary, do me a favor. Just shut up."

It was almost dark, but we finished, clasping each other's hands as we crossed the finish line. Gary forgave my mile twenty-three behavior, and the next year, his wife, Reesa, decided to join us—the three of us raising money for the Michael J. Fox Foundation. Better still, Reesa wasn't a talker.

Running gives you the illusion that you're in charge of your body until your body lets you know otherwise. Caregiving, on the other hand, never offers that fantasy. Instead, it made me feel like I was driving a car that was careening down the highway, with my seatbelt unbuckled and someone next to me grabbing at the steering wheel. Sometimes I wasn't even sure I was in the front seat.

By this time, I knew that caregiving was, among other things, an exercise in acceptance. Eileen and Sinai showed me that, while you could choose how to respond to certain challenges and provocations, it was equally important to understand that whatever you did wouldn't necessarily impact what followed. If my mom kept being grumpy, they mostly just listened and let it go. If she reverted to her sunnier self, they enjoyed the moment and responded to her smile. They knew there were limits to how they could affect either outcome. I knew it, too; I just wasn't good at accepting that reality.

This is why establishing a training regimen matters. A key element of distance training is to give yourself some slack—some days when you don't run; where you don't do anything more strenuous than grin and bear your cumulative aches and pains. I needed to do the same with caregiving. I was doing much better at giving myself breaks and spending time with Lynn, but it was just as crucial to find ways to occasionally give caregiving a rest while I was with my mom.

As much as I loved my mom's old house, it wasn't mine. The small things in life that make you feel settled weren't as available—an early morning cup of coffee when you're all alone and the house is dark and cold. Or that spacious time at night when you can finally put your feet up, pour yourself a drink, and talk to an old friend on the phone or watch a ballgame on TV. I didn't have that quiet sense of being exactly where I wanted to be. That meant I had to be more creative if I was going to give myself a break.

Whenever I was working in San Francisco, I usually took the train back and forth from my mom's home in Menlo Park. Sometimes I'd run late, and I'd walk as fast as I could from the train station in order to begin my shift, as I now usually thought of it. On one such occasion, I was striding down Menlo Park's main street when I passed a local bistro and noticed a basketball game on the TV screen above the bar. And it was not just any basketball game—I could spot this team's cheerleaders and mascot in a blink. It was a University of Wisconsin game, and having spent twenty years of my life in Madison, I was still a huge UW fan. Since it was almost time for me to clock in, I kept walking. About twenty paces later, I stopped. *What the hell?* I went back to the bar, called Eileen to tell her I'd be a little late, ordered a beer (it was a Wisconsin game, after all) and watched the final twenty minutes. The Badgers won.

Taking a short break may not fully recharge your batteries, but it can remind you of who you still are. And taking a few steps, or a few sips, in that direction really matters. Which is another way of saying you need beer for the journey.

My third and fourth marathons were as arduous as the second. I was getting slower and hurting more with each passing year. I was sixty-six when I ran in my fourth New City York Marathon, and I decided that as great an experience as it had been, it would have to be my last.

Long-distance running did more than just increase my physical endurance; it also gave me a new perspective on emotional endurance. I learned that, just as my physical abilities could be stretched, my caregiving capacity didn't have to be fixed either. That didn't mean that caregiving ever got much easier for me. It didn't, any more than I ever made it to mile twenty-three of the New York City Marathon without feeling like my legs were going to fall off. Which, by the way, is why the Michael J. Fox Foundation places a cheering section at that very point.

To have a chance at finishing any marathon, but particularly the one known as caregiving, requires discipline, persistence, and the ability to get used to it. But it also makes an enormous difference to be accompanied—to be joined by those who provide the wind at your back. Which is why, in spite of everything, and because of everything, I would make that run again.

13

THE TWO ADELAIDES

EARLY ONE MORNING in the fall of her 101st year, I found my mom sitting alone in the kitchen. She was wearing her favorite maroon bathrobe, and her walker was perched beside her, angled out into the room. She was uncharacteristically quiet, offering no greeting or comment on the day's news.

She turned toward me, and without preamble, said:

> I think there are two Adelaides.
> There's the good Adelaide—
> the one who's pretty and smart
> and knows how to do things.
> And there's the bad Adelaide—
> the one who's ugly and stupid
> and can't do anything.
>
> I'm not sure which one is here right
> now, but I think it's the bad Adelaide.

I remember taking a deep breath and closing my eyes for a moment, and saying to myself, "Well, here we are."

I don't remember anything else about that morning, including whether my mom and I talked after she made that pronouncement. I think we must have, but I don't know. I just remember having this sense of arrival—that the steady, inexorable drift I'd noticed over the past few years had settled.

Early in my time as a caregiver, I'd talked with my mom's physician about the first subtle softening of her razor-sharp memory.

"Adelaide probably just has what we call age-appropriate dementia," the doctor said.

And I remember thinking, *Well, don't we all?*

But now, not only had we arrived somewhere very different, my mom had announced the arrival herself.

✦

One of the revealing parts of living with someone with dementia is learning what it means and what it doesn't—that cognitive loss and stunning perceptiveness can live side by side. In my mom's case, it seemed to be a state that opened the door to both revelation and darkening fear.

On the morning my mom told me about the two Adelaides, she was still a long way from losing her ability to communicate. Indeed, in that moment, she'd used language to describe her reality with searing incisiveness. And even as memory faded, she could still sharply and matter-of-factly articulate her point of view.

One morning, she summed up her perspective on daily life by saying, "I'm an ordinary person, it seems to me. I don't understand why people find it hard to take care of me."

What was striking, and what was new, was how eloquently artful her statements sometimes became. She'd never been a poetic person, which was why it had been so startling when a few years before, she'd stared at a blank computer screen and said, "It's like looking into a dark river and not being able to see the fish."

And now more of those observations were starting to unfold—statements both keenly insightful and strikingly beautiful.

✦

> I feel like the sun surrounded by clouds.
>
> The sun understands me. It's trying to poke through the gray.
>
> —Adelaide Iverson, age 102

✦

Even as dementia diminished her, my mom's distinguishing characteristics persisted, including her interest in the world around her. Yet because her closeup vision was getting worse, her daily portal to that world, *The New York Times*, was going dark. It was difficult to imagine my mom without a newspaper in her hands, so I continued the subscription anyway. She'd hold up the paper, reading glasses perched on her nose, never letting on that she couldn't read the printed page in front of her.

Eventually, I switched to the large-print edition. But it only came once a week, so I often supplemented it with additional articles I'd print up in large font, complete with the iconic *Times* logo at the top. She'd also kept a detailed calendar all her life, and when she couldn't read it any longer, I got a whiteboard to write out the day's schedule in large letters. Those attempts were worthwhile, which means they worked until they didn't.

My mom wasn't just interested in knowing about the world, she still wanted to participate in it. She could still use a walker around the house, but a wheelchair was necessary to venture out. A neighbor had given us a lightweight transport chair that worked well to get my mom out to the car, but Eileen wanted to make sure we could still take her for walks downtown, so she bought Adelaide an expensive wheelchair for Christmas. I felt what I usually felt about such kindness—both remiss and ever more grateful.

Our usual destination was Peet's Coffee, a half-mile away in downtown Menlo Park. One day, as we headed that way, we came across some lovely hydrangeas bobbing gently in the breeze, and as we passed by, my mom said, "Look at the flowers. They're nodding at me."

And perhaps that same newfound way of looking out into the world is what had inspired another novel activity: she started waving. She waved at everyone and then some. Old people and young, dogs, babies, flags flapping in the wind. Some people smiled. Some waved back. Some looked the other way or never looked up from their screens.

She liked it when people acknowledged her. That, of course, was nothing new. But the waving was. She was especially delighted by small children and dogs.

"Oh, look!" she'd say, as we would wheel by a child.

She had never been effusive with children, even her grandchildren. But now she was. Same for dogs. She loved it when someone stopped with their dog and she could reach out to pet it. The dogs were consistently accommodating—a wag in response to a wave.

Spending time at Peet's Coffee had long been one of our go-to activities. I think she enjoyed being part of the action—sitting there, looking at people and munching on a cookie. We'd count the number of customers coming in and note whether there were more men (the preferred outcome) than women. Once, I asked her if she'd like me to wheel her around so she could take a closer look at all the male customers, and so we did. In previous years, we'd chat about what we saw and what was going on in downtown Menlo Park. But now, we had entered a time where my mom talked less, even as she remained alert to each unfolding moment.

As we were leaving, we passed by a young man working at a laptop. My mom reached out and waved.

He looked up and smiled. "Why, hello."

My mom said, "I like your glasses."

And he said, "Well, thank you very much. I like your coat."

She beamed in response.

I realized that I needed to remember these moments because they are evidence of how simple and dutiful it is to honor the person right in front of you. I needed to remember and appreciate the young man with glasses, and all the others who either, by instinct or experience, knew how to greet someone who's diminished. They're the ones who looked her right in the eye and affirmed that she was still someone.

Yes, they seemed to say with their eyes as much as their words, *I know you count.* There was no faux sweetness, no cooing, no turning to me and saying, "Isn't she sweet?" They only had eyes for her.

✦

My mom may not have been as able to track things as clearly anymore, both cognitively and visually, but that didn't mean she'd lost her passion for Stanford sports. We still went to games, claiming the wheelchair accessible seats.

One evening, we attended a particularly exciting Stanford football game, which they lost in the last seconds. As we wheeled our way out of the stadium, I commented on what a tough loss it had been.

My mom looked at me with a troubled expression. "But I thought we won."

I could have kicked myself, and soon after, decided on an alternative plan. From that point forward, whenever she asked, "Are we ahead?" or "Are we going to win?" the answer was always yes. Stanford went undefeated the rest of the way in football, and they had a perfect record in basketball, too.

✦

When you live with someone with dementia, you live scene by scene, and some scenes aren't as easy to maneuver as manipulating the final score. One day, when she was 102, I walked into my mom's room and took in her intense glare. This wasn't entirely uncommon, and

I rarely knew what sentence might follow. But what she said next was something I never expected to hear.

"David, I know that you were married to someone else before you were married to me."

I've since learned that it's not uncommon for someone with advancing dementia to conflate family members: sons become husbands, wives become daughters. But in that moment, it was stunning.

I paused a long time before responding. And while I knew it wasn't a particularly helpful comment, all I could think to say was, "Mom, I'm not your husband. I'm your son David."

It didn't register.

It was baffling and bewildering, unsettling and mind bending.

One day, she even asked me if I'd like to crawl into bed with her. But in a certain way, her delusionary moments also made complete sense. As much as I loved to joke about my mom's preference for male company, it was much more than that. She wanted a man. She wanted a husband. And she'd take me. After all, in her view, I was available. Her body and mind may have begun to shrink, but her essential core was still there. She'd always wanted a man by her side, and she wanted one now. My mom hadn't gone away; she'd just become a starker, more concentrated version of her earlier self.

+

I'd never known much about my mom's history with men. Only that there'd been one serious candidate before my dad—a fellow named Bob Adams, who wanted to marry her. But neither set of parents approved for religious reasons. He was Presbyterian; my mom Catholic. My dad, on the other hand, was agnostic and agreeable, which was apparently preferable. The children would be raised Catholic. Plus, there was a war going on.

From the moment she met my dad, Adelaide was never interested in anyone else. But she still loved male attention, especially from younger men. When my daughter, Laura, was getting married, she'd designated her cousin Jens to be my mom's escort. My mom adored Jens, and I thought she'd be thrilled to take the arm of her grandson. But right before the wedding, she confided in me that she'd had her eye on another candidate—a handsome young man named Asad, who was one of Laura's best friends, and part of the wedding party as well. Still, she graciously made do.

It's not that my mom didn't have deep and lasting friendships with many women. Her best friends were remarkable women. But she had an internal tuning fork that vibrated a bit differently around men. And even now—or perhaps, especially now—when it was tougher to exert her primacy, the desire for male attention remained. That singular aspect of her personality usually prompted a shake of the head or a smile, but it could also produce pain. That's what happened one evening to Lynn.

My mom had always liked Lynn, dating back to the time when we were teenagers. But now, her usual warmth and affection could sometimes be displaced by outright resentment, as if she viewed Lynn as competition for my time and affection.

On this particular occasion, Lynn was at the house, along with Paul and Yoko, and I asked her if she'd go sit with my mom and keep her and Paul and Yoko company while I made dinner. Later that night, Lynn described what happened next. She tried to make conversation, telling Adelaide the latest about her three children.

But Adelaide replied, "Some people think everything is about them."

Lynn tried again, this time asking Adelaide about her various friends and when she'd be seeing them next.

Her response was, "Some people don't really care about others, even if they try to sound like they do."

Yoko looked at Lynn with a pained expression and then looked down at the floor.

There was a long pause, and then Lynn said quitely, "Adelaide, are you talking about me?"

But Adelaide just glared straight ahead. Finally, Lynn got up and left the room.

+

Over the next year and a half, her confusion over who I was would play out many times, often with desperate pleading. As my mom's sense of the past faded, she became that much more bewildered by the present.

> **Adelaide**: I want you to like me.
>
> **Me**: I do like you. You're my mom.
>
> **Adelaide**: Please don't say that.
>
> **Me**: But you are my mom. I'm
> your son.
>
> **Adelaide**: Please, please don't say that.
>
> —Adelaide, age 102, July 2015

Sometimes I'd try to boost her ego by reminding her of her own wonderful accomplishments. Once, I brought out the letters she'd received from the Stanford football, basketball, and baseball coaches on her hundredth birthday. I read them to her, one by one.

She looked at me and said, "But they didn't write to me today."

✦

The best advice I've ever heard about living scene by scene came from Michael J. Fox, whose foundation has made a huge difference in the lives of people with Parkinson's. In learning to contend with the disease's daily challenges, Fox often refers to a rule he first learned as an actor. Actors, he says, must always focus on playing the scene they're in. Actors have a script, so they know how the show ends, but they can't play a particular scene with that knowledge in mind. They can only play the scene they're in. So it is, Fox observes, with living with Parkinson's disease, or any other challenging life circumstance. We may think we know how the script will end, but we have to focus on the present moment and act within it. And if we do, then that will lead us to the next scene, whatever it may be.

I would try to remember to follow that sage advice, but our caregiver Roanet Morales also offered a useful corollary. Her approach was to just change the scenery.

I remember her once opening the front door, and before even stepping through, saying, "Adelaide!" (She always said Adelaide with an exclamation point.) "Adelaide! Let's go see some flowers."

And before my mom could say a word, Roanet wheeled her out of the house, and they were off to a nearby rose garden. If Roanet had inched her way into the idea, or broached it with less enthusiasm, I don't think it would have happened.

I've never been good at living by exclamation points, but Roanet taught me that sometimes we need them.

One day, I decided to follow Roanet's example. "We're going to the beach," I announced.

My mom had always loved the ocean. We'd taken the same drive as a family for sixty years, over La Honda Road and heading toward Highway 1. When I was a kid, we'd always compete to see who could spot the ocean first. Today, as we approached the old San Gregorio General Store, the ocean came into view, a mile or so away.

My mom wasn't able to see it, so I said, "I have to keep my eyes on the road, Mom, so let me know when you see the ocean."

About a hundred feet from the water, she exclaimed, "I see it!" And a wide smile creased her face.

We were at the point when I wanted us both to savor these moments, precisely because I knew they wouldn't last, that moments can't be banked or reclaimed later when you need a good-moment credit.

I knew I would remember this trip, and that she might not. In fact, I knew that later that day, she might complain that she hadn't been to the ocean for a long time. When similar exchanges had taken place in the past, I'd often reminded her, sometimes pleadingly, of whatever we'd just done. I no doubt sounded like a kid trying to convince a parent she was wrong. Probably because I *was* a kid trying to convince a parent she was wrong.

But as we drove toward the water on this beautiful spring day, I tried to remember to do better. To just play the scene I was in. To take in the joy I saw on her face, precisely because it would only be experienced then. For her, there wouldn't be a later savoring. I tried to remember that moments are to be treasured because they do not last. Like a cloud pushed by the wind, moments part as they become.

Today we're driving south from San Gregorio, along Highway 1. There are prettier spots on the coast road, but none imbued with so much memory. As always, we pulled to a stop at Pescadero State Beach, our ocean destination for the past sixty years. Nobody in my family knows why this is true. Bean Hollow, a few miles further south, is prettier. Pomponio, a few miles to the north, affords longer walks along the cliffs. But Pescadero is home.

We pulled into the parking lot just south of the beach because it offers the best view from inside the car. We sat and watched, and we were quiet.

As we were parked there, I happened to notice that the children's book *The Little Engine That Could* was on the back seat. I'd recently purchased one of those classic editions to take back east to read to my three-year-old granddaughter. I don't know why, but I asked my mom if she wanted me to read it to her, and she said yes. Maybe she liked the title since she was always someone who thought she could, too, and was deeply annoyed when events transpired to obstruct her daily mission: you get up in the morning and you do what needs to be done, for the good of family and the good of society. And you do not stop.

For my mom, getting old didn't include giving herself a pass. Accepting limitations was not within her DNA. It was her greatest strength, and now, sometimes, the source of her greatest pain—a pain that she would sometimes inflict on others. But in that moment, I read her a story, and together we took in the sound of the words, the wind, and the waves.

What I didn't realize was that this would be the last time we'd ever make that journey.

14

IT'S TIME

A FEW MONTHS LATER, I was looking out at a different sea, surrounded by Maine's rocky coast. I was standing on a place we called the ledges, near the village of Five Islands. I had rented a house in the village for the next two weeks.

Time changes for me when I'm in Maine, a place where the daily rhythm is defined by the tides and the sound of lobster boats heading out to sea. I stood on an outcropping of metamorphic rock formed more than four hundred million years ago—a series of ledges folded together, angling upward. The breeze was stiff, the waves loud. There was no place I'd rather be.

I fell in love with the state of Maine in the late 1990s, when my daughter, Laura, attended Bates College, an excellent liberal arts institution located in Lewiston, an old mill town that flourished in the nineteenth century, and has struggled ever since. But Lewiston isn't far from Maine's spectacular coast. And now, thanks to Eileen,

Sinai, and Roanet, I could be here for longer, with Lynn joining me for my second week. All in all, it was a glorious prospect.

A few days after I left Menlo Park, I got a call from Eileen. My mom had fallen. She'd pushed herself up out of the wheelchair while Eileen was in the bathroom, and used her walker to negotiate her way toward the front door. She probably intended to go for a walk, but fell instead.

They'd gone to the doctor, and X-rays revealed a broken collarbone. Adelaide was doing OK, Eileen told me, but she was a little discouraged. She'd be in a sling for six weeks, which meant she could no longer use a walker around the house and would need to rely on a wheelchair instead.

I was concerned and called her doctor. Dr. Steve Lai was a palliative care specialist who'd taken over my mom's care the year before and made monthly home visits. He told me he thought she could recover, and hopefully regain her strength. I asked him if he thought I should come home. To my relief, he said no.

And then I called a good friend who was a retired nurse, and asked her to go by the house to see how everyone was faring. Kathleen called me later to say that all was well, and that Adelaide was annoyed that she'd come to check on her. This convinced me she was fine.

And so my Maine idyll continued. I called my mom regularly, of course, and she mostly sounded OK. But then something shifted. She sounded more discouraged, and Eileen told me she'd begun to worry.

"She misses you, David."

I asked again if I should come home, and not surprisingly, Eileen knew the answer I wanted to hear.

"No. You don't have to come."

And I didn't.

A few days later, Eileen called to say that she was getting really worried about Adelaide.

"She's too quiet. She's not responding."

We decided that Eileen should take her to see the doctor again. I was heading home the next day, anyway.

The next afternoon, I was at JFK Airport, waiting for my flight home to San Francisco, when my phone rang.

"David," Dr. Lai said. "You told me to call you if I thought you should come home. And it's time. I'm so sorry to tell you this, but I don't think your mom has much longer to live."

I couldn't believe it. It didn't seem possible to me that a moment I had imagined many times, and longed for more than once, was actually happening. A single tear drifted down my cheek. I asked the only question that occurred to me.

"How long?"

"A few weeks," he replied. "I think you should begin hospice care. And if it's OK with you, I'll have the hospice team go over to the house tonight."

I told him I was on my way.

✦

I arrived that evening, on a dark, clear October night, and I noticed smoke curling out of the chimney. I smiled. My mom loved a fire.

When I got inside, she was sitting next to the fireplace in her wheelchair, sporting a black sling but wearing a favorite blazer, with a blanket over her legs. She looked up as I walked over to her. I bent down to hug her gently and to tell her I loved her. She smiled. She was quiet but seemed OK. And then I hugged Eileen, and she gave me the latest update.

While at the doctor's office, the staff had taken a urine sample, and they'd just gotten the results—another UTI. I instantly wondered if that was the sole cause of my mom's rapid decline. Past UTIs had knocked her for a loop. Maybe she needed antibiotics, not hospice.

And at the same time that thought arrived, so did another: *Do I want this to be another treatable UTI? Or am I actually hoping that we are nearing the end?*

The next morning, I called Dr. Lai and asked him if the UTI was the real cause of my mom's decline, and whether antibiotics would not only take care of the infection, but also extend her life.

"No," he replied in a gentle tone. "The medication will just make her comfortable. Perhaps it means she'll live a few weeks more than I'd originally thought. But it won't be more than that. It's just that time, Dave. I'm sorry."

He was sorry. But was I?

I was awash in emotions, but mostly I was filled with a sweet sadness and an intense desire to do right by her. To see her through.

✦

Like most people, I suspect, I had only a vague notion of what hospice provided. I knew it wasn't usually a place, but rather a set of services that came to you. But it turns out, hospice provides much more than I had realized: doctor visits as needed; a weekly nursing visit; a home health aide who would come twice a week to help with personal care (including the still important shampoo and hair care); all needed prescriptions; plus supplies like gloves, adult diapers, and wipes. They'd even replace her current hospital bed, and it would all be covered by Medicare. There are certainly many things wrong with the American health-care system, but having hospice as a Medicare benefit is not one of them.

We built many fires that fall, and we had many sweet moments. Once, when I was sitting next to her, Adelaide looked up at me and said with great clarity and focus, "What do you think it will be like?"

My mom had never talked much about death, always telling me instead how much she wanted to live. But I wondered if that was changing, too.

"Do you mean what happens when we die?" I said.

She nodded.

I hadn't thought about what I would say to that question, and so I just started talking, trying to just be true to whatever emotions welled up inside me. I told her I wasn't too sure about heaven, but I thought that wherever she was going would be warm and sunny, and that there might be baseball, and that I was pretty sure there would be love.

I kept on in this vein for a while, and then suddenly my mom said, "Oh, quit talking."

And I laughed.

Then I said, "Well, Mom, I don't know if you're ready for whatever comes next. but I sure hope they're ready for you."

✦

One late October morning, my mom told me she saw Christmas trees.

"Do you mean you saw them on TV?" I said.

"No. I see them because I like how they make me feel." And then she said, "Is it Christmas?"

To which I replied, "Do you want it to be?"

And she said yes.

I went outside and cut down a volunteer pine tree that was growing in the side yard. I put the tree in the Christmas tree stand and put up the same decorations my mom had used for the past sixty years. And then Eileen and I put up all the old family Christmas cards dating back to when my folks moved into the house in 1950—cards that featured black and white photos of my brothers and me as kids, sitting in a living room that still looked exactly the same.

My mom sat by the tree, eyes closed, the evergreen branches framing her wheelchair, a maroon throw blanket crocheted by a friend tucked under her chin. Another Christmas like so many. Only this time, it was Christmas in October.

✦

My mom grew steadier after a ten-day course of antibiotics, seeming stronger both physically and mentally. But the hospice nurse and our doctor didn't think that foreshadowed any lasting change. Time was short, they counseled gently, and we should encourage those who want to see her to come.

And they did. Grandchildren came from far away, as did other friends and relatives. I treasure those photos of so many smiling faces, including my mom's as she held a new autographed basketball given to her by the Stanford team.

There's one photo from that time that remains particularly bittersweet. It happened when Paul and Yoko's daughter, Ayuko, came to visit from New York City, where she was in the middle of her medical residency at Mt. Sinai Hospital. My mom had played a central role in Ayuko's early years, picking her up at school and bringing her back to the Menlo Park home, a place Ayuko always loved. Her cousins, aunts, and uncles were all either on the other side of the country, or the other side of the world in Japan, and I think my mom provided an all-encompassing love and a deep sense of home that was foundational to who Ayuko would become.

I have a beautiful picture of her visit during that Christmas in October—the two of them sitting side by side, embracing. My mom beaming at the granddaughter she adored, and Ayuko equally radiant, her eyes shining with tears.

The day after that lovely visit, I said to my mom, "Wasn't it great to see Ayuko?"

She replied with authority, "Well, I'm sorry I missed her. She must have come when I wasn't here."

I don't remember what I said in response. Hopefully I had enough sense not to dispute her account. But I don't think memory is the only measure of what matters. That moment mattered to Ayuko, and it mattered to me. And most importantly, it mattered to Adelaide when it happened. The fact that she didn't recall it a day later is only testimony to what she can retain, not to who she'd always be.

As the author Christian Wiman observes, our life experience doesn't really matter until it becomes "catalyzed in the lives of others." And Adelaide was nothing if not catalytic.

+

One of the many lessons I learned that fall was the importance of showing up—something brought home to me by family and friends: Paul, Yoko, Lynn, Kathleen, Susan, Lora, Nancy, Laurie, Joanie, Louise, Mary Jane, Ed, Kiki, Michael, Doug, Peggy, Dan, Cynthia, Gary, Reesa, Gerry, and Mary. They came to visit without fail. They understood that Adelaide could still pack a punch, and that their visits could be greeted with a bark as easily as a smile. But they loved her for who she'd been and who she still wanted to be.

And no one showed up more consistently than Sinai and Eileen. They were always there, through all the long days and nights. Sometimes we'd sit together by her bed late at night, the room illuminated only by a nightlight, sharing a memory or sharing the silence, with Adelaide at the center, presenting the many faces of human need: hunger and thirst, cold and heat, wetness and worry. And Eileen and Sinai's ability to respond to each never ceased. I watched as they offered a spoonful of food or changed a diaper, bathed her forehead or tucked in a blanket, all with the same gentle firmness. It reminded me of my own shortcomings. But it also reminded me of my aspirations.

I made lists of when to give her six ounces of Ensure—a milkshake-like drink that provides essential vitamins—or the four ounces of juice we mixed with thickener so that she could swallow it. I kept a meticulous schedule of when to give her various medications aimed at reducing agitation and helping her rest. Even at this stage, I must have felt that keeping the schedule straight might impact what would happen next.

Sometimes I saw Eileen making notes late at night as well. I found that reassuring—Eileen was keeping track, too.

✦

In that gentle late-night light, my mom's features seemed to soften. As she lost weight, the flesh receded and her wrinkles smoothed. Her face subtly reformed, taking on the more angular features of her youth—her jawline firm and thrust forward, her nose more prominent. She was really quite beautiful.

I didn't feel regret. I didn't feel relief. I just felt like I was where I wanted to be.

Late one night, I peeked into my mom's bedroom before entering. Eileen was sitting by her side, with her back to me. I watched for a moment before I realized that Eileen was wearing her prayer shawl and holding her Muslim prayer beads. She was murmuring softly in Hindi. I backed away.

The next morning, I told Eileen how touched I was by what I'd seen.

She smiled widely. "Well, Sinai taught me the Lord's Prayer, so sometimes I say that, too."

15

LIFE SUPPORT

TODAY, ADELAIDE IS STRONGER. This morning, she told me, "I haven't done enough good yet."

> And Eileen said that when she apologized to Adelaide for how she used to push her to do her exercises, Adelaide's response was, "It's OK. You made me stronger. And who knows, maybe I'll still surprise you."
>
> So now what? I guess I just have to buckle up and go along for the ride. And yet, I have to say, I was ready for this to end. And I felt Adelaide was ready, too.
>
> —October 31, 2015

✦

My mom appeared to be intent on pulling off her version of that pre-election phenomenon known as an October surprise. A full month after beginning hospice, she was gaining strength rather than losing it. I talked to the hospice doctor and nurse about what was happening. As they got to know my mom, they were becoming more circumspect about what lay ahead. I think they were both humbled and impressed with the ability of a 103-year-old to rally once more. It was clear that we had to move on from celebrating Christmas in October to getting ready for an actual Thanksgiving in November, and I struggled to accept that the future—my future—might just be a continuation of the present.

✦

> I have to say that I'm depressed that Adelaide is still with us. And that's difficult to get my arms around—both that prospect and my own emotions about it.... I've felt good about being here every night once I got the doctor's call. And I've liked being part of all these moments, from witnessing a Muslim prayer to Christmas in October. But the truth is, I'm not really writing this story.
>
> We're not building toward a lovely well-timed conclusion where all the parts come together like some piece of music

that ends on the right chord.
It's more like an extended coda.
And we really have no idea how
or when it will end. And so once
again, I'm facing the *Now what?*
question. It's not that I have
trouble acknowledging how I
feel. Nor do I feel remiss about
feeling down about this. What
I don't know is what to do with
that feeling.

—November 15, 2015

+

My nephew Jens flew in from the Netherlands to spend Thanksgiving with his beloved grandma. We gathered around the Thanksgiving table—the kind of family occasion my mom had presided over for sixty-five years. Same traditional meal, same dining room table, same place settings, same blessing. I imagine most everyone was thinking it would be our last Thanksgiving with Adelaide. Everyone except, perhaps, Adelaide herself, Eileen, and me.

Partway through dinner, Eileen caught my eye and nodded toward Adelaide. She was trying to feed herself—the first time she had picked up a spoon since before she broke her collarbone two months before.

+

And so 2015 is now approaching
2016. Gary called to tell me
that I better start preparing

for Adelaide's 104th birthday. I wasn't amused. And it underlines that my being down about Adelaide continuing to live is really about me and not about her.

Sure, I can rationalize this and say, "It's not really what she would have wanted," or "She won't have much quality of life," but that's not really the issue, and may not even be true.... No, if I'm honest, what brings me down is the prospect of my quality of life, not hers. And it makes me realize that to too great a degree, I've tied the idea of being able to resume my own life with the end of hers. Maybe that's my mom's latest lesson. At least I know enough not to say it will be the last.

—December 2015

+

So instead of the story ending, another chapter was beginning. And I couldn't help but wonder if that should have been the case. What would have happened if we hadn't treated my mom's UTI? In hindsight, it now seemed clear that when Dr. Lai saw a 103-year-old patient who looked like she only had a few weeks to live, he was actually seeing a 103-year-old patient who just happened to have another UTI. If I had known then what I knew now, would it have been better if I had rejected antibiotics and just asked that my mom be kept comfortable?

Antibiotics hardly seem like a heroic measure. It wasn't like I was choosing to place her on a ventilator. But when someone is 103, should we begin to define heroic measures in a different way?

To their credit, my parents had completed both a will and an advanced health-care directive while still in their late seventies. But the questions I now worried about were ones no document or official form could possibly cover—decisions about the steps that should or shouldn't be taken to prolong the life of someone who's 103. At best, a living will or health-care directive only provides a preamble to the bigger questions we face. Questions like: What do we really want to have happen at the end of our lives? How would we like to live, and how would we like to die? What exactly should be done to extend the former or ease the latter?

In my mom's case, we at least had a pretty recent record documenting her views on the basics. Six years earlier, when she was ninety-seven, she and I had gone to an attorney to review and update her advanced directive, and to designate me as both her trust executor and her primary agent for health care. Until then, my older brother held the former role, and the two of us shared the latter. But after talking to my mom and my brothers, we all agreed it made sense for me to take the lead on both.

When we got to the attorney's office, he wisely had me step outside so that he could talk to my mom and make sure this was what she wanted done. And at ninety-seven, she'd been fully able to verify her desires. When it came to updating her advanced directive instructions, she made it clear that her views hadn't changed since she'd filled out the last one, twenty years before. She felt that if she had what the form called, an irreversible condition, she didn't want to depend on life support to keep living. She'd marked the Withhold Treatment box with authority.

But now we'd entered a different time, where checked boxes seemed either too simplistic, no longer relevant, or both. Once you enroll in hospice, you forego the option to call 911 or head for the ER because the program's purpose is to extend quality of life, not its length.

Besides, the questions we now faced were more nuanced. They couldn't be readily answered using medicalized terms like an *irreversible condition,* because when you reach the age of 103, you already *have* an irreversible condition. And what's typically meant by *life-support treatments* is no longer relevant either. We didn't need to make decisions about using a defibrillator or ventilator; we needed to make decisions about antibiotics.

A UTI may be reversible, but treating it with antibiotics extends the life of someone who has an irreversible condition: age itself. Does that make antibiotics a heroic measure? And if so, would my mom now want that? What about using a catheter?

On another recent occasion, my mom hadn't been able to urinate for nearly twenty-four hours. We called hospice, and a nurse came out to insert a catheter, but the procedure was invasive and painful, and ultimately didn't work.

Finally, nature took its course. But was inserting a catheter heroic? It certainly didn't seem to be comfort care. Perhaps it was neither. And shadowing all of these questions was the most crucial one: What would my mom want?

Her long-standing ability to comprehend complex questions and answer them authoritatively was no longer readily present.

These questions aren't reducible to forms and boxes. And as 2016 began, Eileen and Sinai and I would stay up late talking about them. I'd also muse with close friends and family members. Sometimes we'd talk about what *quality of life* really meant. But that only led to the question of, *Who gets to answer?* Or more precisely, *Which Adelaide gets to answer?*

I knew how an earlier Adelaide would have felt about a life without solid food, good Scotch, conversation, *The New York Times,* or Stanford basketball games.

"Oh, come on," that Adelaide would have said. "No way."

But now? From my point of view, my mom didn't have much quality of life. At age 103½, she could no longer walk, see very well, eat the kind of food she loved, or remember the names of her grandchildren. She was a proud woman who wore diapers and hated it when they had to be changed, especially when I was the one doing the changing—not because I was her son, but because I wasn't skilled. But did she still want to live? Yes. Yes, she did.

Did that mean she thought her life had sufficient quality? I had no idea. Especially when she would still look me in the eye and say clearly, "I don't want to die."

Eventually, of course, many of us will find ourselves in some version of this circumstance. We are going to get grayer and slower. We're going to become less nimble, both physically and mentally. We're not going to see as well or do as much. We're not going to be able to continue to read, or run, or travel. We will sleep less well and have less sex. We will lose the people we love. And right now, our present selves would say those losses would vastly reduce our quality of life. But that's not the question we have to try to answer. The question isn't, *What constitutes quality of life now?* The question is, *What quality of life would you find acceptable at some indeterminate age, well into the future?*

Thinking about this has made me realize that just filling out an advanced-care directive for myself and calling it a day—or a life, for that matter—isn't sufficient. I needed to leave behind more than a form in a file folder. I needed to ask myself questions that are more personally complex than just choosing or refusing a particular medical device or treatment. I needed to write about not just my medical preferences, but articulate, with specificity, my end-of-life desires and the values that I wanted to guide those decisions. Precisely because we can't foresee every circumstance, let alone anticipate our own future feelings, I needed to write down the core beliefs and principles I would want to guide my dying days.

But I didn't have that kind of statement from my mom. And in the time we had remaining, it would be up to me to make the best decision I could about the treatments we might or might not employ, and what would most honor the life before me.

16

FIRE IN WINTER

THE WINTER OF 2016 GROUND ON, and that meant I had to do more than just contemplate questions surrounding end-of-life care. I also had to grapple with the nitty-gritty reality of what came next for my mom and me. I had to accept that if my mom regained strength, she might well live for many more months—perhaps even a year or more. Was I still OK spending four or five nights a week in Menlo Park, plus providing twenty hours a week of daytime care?

I had already fashioned as good a circumstance, both personally and professionally, as any family caregiver could reasonably expect. I had the company and camaraderie of my caregiving companions, Eileen and Sinai, and the constancy of Lynn. My finished film *Capturing Grace* had screened at film festivals around the country, and would soon air nationally on PBS. I'd just vacationed in Maine, for God's sake. What wasn't there to like about my life? And I felt grateful for all of those advantages and the added strength they'd given me as a care provider. And yet—I found myself saying those two words a lot—here we were once more, our journey continuing, another year beginning.

So despite my good fortune, despite being buoyed by so much support, I grappled with knowing that my mom would continue to be the fulcrum upon which my life tipped back and forth. As long as I still lived there, every action I contemplated and choice I made would be governed by that vantage point. And as the winter days stretched out in front of me, I felt something I rarely felt: old.

It had been almost twelve years since my original Parkinson's diagnosis, and thanks to good care, good luck, the right meds, and plenty of exercise, I was still doing well. In the Parkinson's world, I was what's known as an outlier—a descriptor for those Parkinson's patients whose disease progresses slowly, and whose symptoms are outside the normal range.

But I also knew that my dad had done well for more than a dozen years, too. Gradually though, his voice had started to grow still, and his body had begun to further stiffen, until finally he could no longer move at all. And my brother, who was in his early seventies, had now had Parkinson's for nearly twenty-five years. He'd already lived with the disease longer than my dad. Peter was still resolute, but I knew Parkinson's haunted his days. I was the lucky Iverson, though I knew I shouldn't count on extended immunity.

And so despite my good fortune and all that I learned alongside Sinai and Eileen, I often felt more than a little bleak about the prospect of so many caregiving tomorrows.

The hard truth was that I was approaching sixty-eight years of age, and I was still living with my mom. To put it more bluntly, my mom and I were two Social Security and Medicare beneficiaries living together. The breaks that used to feel rejuvenating no longer did. Spending the weekend at Lynn's had once felt like a get-out-of-jail-free card. But as the winter wore on, it felt more like a weekend pass that might get revoked at any moment. A wonderful break in Maine, or the deep satisfaction of making my last film, didn't seem to be enough to sustain a life orientation that stayed above the half-full line. Instead, a slow weariness would settle over me as soon as I walked back through my mom's front door. I'd secured just about every lifeline a caregiver can receive, and yet I still felt that I might not ever become untethered.

Those feelngs didn't invalidate the fulfilment I'd experienced as a caregiver. It just illustrates that, even in the best of circumstances, the weariness that accompanies caregiving never goes away.

I was struggling, despite the caregiving capacity I'd gained, to bring my whole heart to the endeavor. I now knew that even when I'd felt a turning point was about to happen—indeed, should happen and must happen—it may not. And that includes the biggest turning point of all—death itself.

Instead of approaching the end of life, we were actually returning to it. Perhaps as long as you're a caregiver, there are no true turning points. There are only commas.

+

I was at the age when your approach to life ought to be well-established. But I found myself fighting not to succumb to a bleaker worldview. In the past, even during challenging times with my mom, I'd been able to rediscover a positive outlook—to find new ways to contend with things that were difficult or demanding. But now, as my mom continued to live, and I needed to be at my best, I wasn't. I didn't always want to make the effort.

Eileen and Sinai seemed to have reserves of goodwill that I either couldn't access, or no longer wanted to find. They accepted both her limitations and her resilience with equal grace, while I once again grew smaller and colder inside.

Throughout those winter months of 2016, my mom continued to grow stronger, and I continued to struggle to accept that reality. I could resume taking her out in the wheelchair for short walks around the neighborhood, though I often didn't feel like it. And Sinai was able to transfer her from the wheelchair into her car to take her for short drives and even to church. She was more able to both speak and be heard, and the sentence that she said most frequently continued to be, "I don't want to die."

One evening, I was building a fire for my mom—something she'd always loved. As I bent over the fireplace, she kept insisting that Sinai hadn't taken her to church, when I knew that she had.

"Sinai didn't take me," she said, over and over.

I would tell her again and again that Sinai had. Back and forth we went, until something in me snapped.

I turned around and shouted at her, "Sinai *did* take you to church! You just don't remember!"

My mom didn't say a word in response. She just hung her head. I knew better, of course, than to erupt in anger—an act no more useful than shouting at someone with Parkinson's whose hand won't stop shaking. I knew better, and yet I couldn't stop myself.

I remember turning back to the fire and staring into the flames, wondering yet again who I was becoming.

+

My friend Gary, who often kept me from feeling too noble, had once said to me, "You know, it's not unusual for someone to take care of their mom. It's just unusual when a white guy does it."

And now here I was, an aging white guy whose life had been blessed by opportunity and open doors from the moment I was born right through my entire experience as a caregiver. Yet I was unable to draw strength from any of that. All I knew, as I stared into the fire, was that I was still here.

I don't remember what kind of night I had. Perhaps it was long and bleak and restless. Perhaps I was exhausted and slept. But in the coming days, I felt a shift inside me. I knew something I had not known before: I had played out my scenes as a primary caregiver, and I knew what I had to do. I had to walk out the front door and come back not as a caregiver, but as a son. I knew it with such interior clarity that I felt eager, rather than reluctant, to tell Eileen and Sinai.

And so we talked. I told them that I couldn't keep doing what I was doing. I didn't want any more three-bell nights. I couldn't do this impossible, gratifying, excruciating, and life-changing job anymore. I just didn't want to. To my everlasting gratitude, they understood.

And so they took charge. They changed their own schedules and recruited friends so that I no longer had to cover the nights. Now, when I went to bed, it would be in my dad's old study located in the back of the house, rather than in my childhood bedroom ten feet down the hall from my mom.

I still remember the first night I headed to my new sleeping quarters and closed the door—something I hadn't done in years.

✦

Over the next several months, I would gradually reduce how much time I spent at my mom's, and I felt OK with the choice I had made. I didn't feel regret, not even about not being able to go the full distance. I think it was because I realized that I didn't have to be a hero. I had two people—the two best people—who would be there for me. My mom was still central to my life, that would never change. But my position had shifted. Thanks to Eileen and Sinai, I could step to the side without stepping away.

It's often said that America is a nation of immigrants. But in that moment, and in many more, Eileen and Sinai forever altered my understanding of what that actually means. They were women who'd arrived in America with nothing but skill, determination, and a deep cultural understanding that caring for the old is part of life's bargain. And while the Statue of Liberty may beckon to those who arrive tempest tossed and yearning to breathe free, Eileen and Sinai taught me that it also works the other way around—that sometimes it's America's newest arrivals who offer that comforting embrace.

When I was at my lowest moment, it was Sinai and Eileen who provided me with safe harbor. They helped me realize that the Statue of Liberty's invitation is issued to all of us, and that when we hold true to that promise, we strengthen our sense of family and the fabric of American life.

III

LAST CALL

17

GOOD WILL

I FELT DIFFERENT IN ALMOST EVERY WAY from that point forward. My change of circumstance altered how I went to bed at night and how I got up in the morning. And perhaps most fundamentally, it altered my relationship with my mom. It allowed me to be both more affectionate and more distant at the same time. I could kiss my mom on the cheek and then say good night. I could sit beside her and offer her spoonfuls of thickened juice, but not attempt to change a diaper. I could leave. I could close the door behind me. In a sense, I felt like I'd returned to who I once was. I felt like a son.

Throughout the spring and summer of 2016, Sinai and Eileen helped reawaken that part of me which had periodically grown numb. They reminded me of how best to respond when someone no longer always makes sense. How to bring care and compassion to the most elemental of human tasks: the spooning of food, the cleansing of skin, the tenderness of a simple touch. They renewed my awareness of the miracle of continuing kindness. And I realized that what my mom had said three years before was fundamentally right: there was another Adelaide.

But while she had defined the two Adelaides by their personality, physicality, and liveliness of mind, I saw a different Adelaide now—one whose remarkable will had merged with the bonds of affection that enfolded her.

✦

Every Thursday morning, I now drove from Lynn's house north of Berkeley, down to my mom's in Menlo Park, and stayed until Friday afternoon. After I got back to Lynn's, I'd spend the entire weekend there before I set back out Monday morning for another overnight stay. And then I'd repeat the cycle. I still believed in the importance of schedules, and this was perfect. I lived with Lynn, but twice a week I was able to visit—and using that word makes all the difference—my mom. I could still give Eileen and Sinai breaks, take my mom for walks in her wheelchair, read to her in the early evenings, or sit by her side late at night. I could do all that, but I'd also begun a life with Lynn. That gave me the grace and goodwill to do what I'd always said I wanted—to see my mom through.

I also had more enthusiasm for tackling caregiving's ongoing challenges—probably because I wouldn't be living with the consequences of whatever solutions I concocted. And we had some serious challenges to figure out, starting with where the money was going to come from to cover the care I had been providing—care that was necessary both for my mom's sake and my own. But at least I now had a clear delineation of my role. Now I was a son who helped coordinate caregiving.

That additional care wasn't going to cost what extraordinary care inside a hospital might, but make no mistake, it was still extraordinary care. After all, it wasn't new advances in treatment or sophisticated devices that had nurtured my mom back to life. It was antibiotics, coupled with hospice and Eileen and Sinai's skill and compassion.

As Dr. Atul Gawande observed in his book *Being Mortal,* American medicine tends to focus on "the repair of health, not sustenance of the soul." But Sinai and Eileen were entirely focused on a singular human soul—well, two souls, actually.

That human focus is, of course, central to what it takes to be a good caregiver. But if you'd like a more measurable means to assess quality of care, let me add an additional metric: skin. What does someone's skin look like if they're bedridden?

At age 103, my mom's skin was still beautiful. And so it would remain as long as Eileen and Sinai were present. There were few, if any, blemishes, let alone bed sores. Our wonderful hospice nurse Chris Brady was constantly amazed at how well Adelaide always looked, particularly her skin. And if you ask anyone who's ever been around a nursing home very much, that just doesn't happen. It takes vigilance, tenderness, and skill to keep skin healthy. It means knowing when and how to turn someone in bed, knowing how to spot the first signs of darkening skin, knowing which ointments work and which don't, knowing when to bandage and when not to. That knowledge sustains life as much, if not more, than many sophisticated hospital machines.

And while I still sometimes felt overwhelmed by the prospect of my mom continuing to live indefinitely, there was no way I wanted to change her living circumstances. It wasn't hard to reject extraordinary medical intervention. It might not even be that hard to someday reject an antibiotics prescription. But to take away the extraordinary care that Eileen and Sinai provided? No way.

In the San Francisco Bay Area, this kind of care also carries an extraordinary price tag. And now that I'd taken myself out of the care-provider role pretty much altogether, we were running short on money. The cost of twenty-four-hour-a-day home care in the Bay Area by that time was about $14,000 a month. One year earlier, as we were approaching a zero balance on my mom's $250,000 home equity credit line, I'd gotten the bank to approve an additional $100,000, but they'd told me they wouldn't be able to extend it again. And now we only had enough left to fund a few more months of care.

One option was to seek out government assistance. Medicare doesn't pay for home-based care or long-term nursing care, but if you've spent down all your assets, you can try to qualify for need-based assistance through the state. In California, there's a program called Medi-Cal that pays for facility based care, but I was conflicted about that possibility. First, of course, I wanted to keep my mom at home. Second, while Medi-Cal doesn't factor home ownership into their eligibility equation, it didn't seem right that someone who owned such a valuable piece of real estate should be able to receive need-based assistance. And even if I'd been able to get over my moral qualms, there was also a practical consideration: while owning a valuable home doesn't preclude someone from qualifying for assistance, the state can come back later and ask the estate to repay those benefits once the home is eventually sold. I didn't want to deal with that either.

Another possibility was to move my mom to a long-term care facility and then rent the house to generate the income to pay for that care. Eileen suggested an additional alternative: I could rent the house, but she would take Adelaide home with her to Tracy, some seventy miles to the east. Her costs would be substantially less than a care facility, and the care she provided would be more skilled and far more personal.

Over the next month, I visited a half-dozen nursing homes and thought long and hard about Eileen's offer. The nursing homes were mostly OK. I met good people, and I knew my mom would be professionally cared for. But it wouldn't be home. Nor would she get anything close to the amount of personal care she currently received, or would receive, if I moved her to Eileen's. Remember: skin care.

But the truth was that I wasn't happy about either prospect. The institutional nature of having my mom in a long-term care facility was deeply unappealing, and this was before COVID-19. And while I knew she would do much better at Eileen's, it was also a long ways away. I knew I'd go see her once a week, but probably not more, and I didn't like the idea of that much distance between us. I felt stuck.

And then I started thinking about another possibility. I could pull money out of my savings to pay for her care, knowing that I would eventually be repaid when my mom's house sold. I might even be able to extend the timeline further if I asked Eileen and Sinai to work for a reduced rate and be repaid in full at a later date.

I did a quick calculation. If they were amenable, and if I used $50,000 from my savings, that plus my mom's retirement income could keep her at home for another six months, on into the fall.

Both Eileen and Sinai readily and graciously agreed. My brothers and sisters-in-law were supportive, too. We were OK. At least for now.

Of course, all I was doing was literally buying time. Our plan was, at best, a holding pattern, girded together by Eileen and Sinai's graciousness and goodwill. My contribution was to make the world's most secure loan, guaranteed by my parents' fortuitous home purchase sixty-five years earlier. But it also illustrates where we are as a country when it comes to providing care for the old. If you're blessed with good fortune, you have a chance. But beyond that, we currently have no plan, no national policy, no rational or reasonable way to provide the elements of loving care, let alone extraordinary care, for those approaching the end of life. For now, we rely on hope, fortified by immigrant Americans and happenstance.

✦

My mom would soon turn 104. And by now, the fact that she was still with us was no longer surprising. But that didn't mean she couldn't still prompt some entirely unexpected additional challenges.

One late March day, the furnace quit working. Like

my mom, it had gone well beyond normal life expectancy. But in the end, its inner mechanics were apparently made of less sturdy stuff. Do you buy a new furnace when your mom is on hospice and approaching 104?

In the real-estate-mad Bay Area, the value of my mom's home was based on its address, not the house itself. I knew that it would be sold and then quickly torn down. Did it really make sense to put in a new furnace?

The furnace guy said that our 1950s ducts contained asbestos, and while not harmful currently, today's building codes would require an expensive abatement procedure. Replacing the furnace, removing all the asbestos, and installing new duct work would cost around $15,000. You can contemplate matters of life and death and quality of care all you want, but you still can't avoid the nitty gritty of furnace replacement costs.

The Bay Area is temperate, and the weather was getting warmer, so Eileen, Sinai, and I decided we would limp along, relying on the trusty old fireplace in the living room, plus strategically placed space heaters in my mom's room and elsewhere around the house. We were probably violating twenty-three different city codes, but it felt appropriate just the same. And if Adelaide continued to live until the next winter or beyond...well, there was no way to complete that thought, other than to do what I just did—with an ellipsis.

+

And then another surprising challenge came our way. My mom might soon outlive hospice.

In order to qualify for hospice services, a doctor must certify that a patient isn't expected to live more than six months. If that individual lives beyond that time frame, the hospice team is required to do another assessment and make a new determination.

When our six months had passed and it was time for the first reassessment, the medical director of our hospice service called me and said, with a chuckle, "You know, your mom might become the oldest person we've ever had graduate from hospice care."

I knew that hospice was required to follow certain Medicare eligibility rules, but the thought of losing their assistance was unnerving. There was so much they provided, from weekly nursing visits to needed supplies and medications.

I called my mom's former physician to ask if he would call the medical director to stress how needy my mom still was, and how crucial the family viewed hospice care. I don't know whether his call made a difference, but thankfully, we got a temporary reprieve.

From that point forward, however, hospice recertification would take place every three months. And as we approached the next reassessment, I was worried that it would be increasingly difficult to make the case that my mom still qualified. Sure, she was nearly 104, but vital signs? Her blood oxygen level was excellent, and her blood pressure averaged around 120/70—numbers people half her age would be delighted to have. Lungs? Totally clear. Bed sores? Nary a one.

A kind and gentle hospice nurse practitioner named Anna Woods came to the house to do the next assessment. She took her vitals, and then I watched as she measured the circumference of my mom's arms. It was one of the few ways they could document weight loss for patients who could no longer stand on a scale. Her arms had shrunk by a half-inch.

Anna looked at me. "Well, she's continuing to lose weight. I'll see if I can make a case to continue her on service."

Months later, our regular hospice nurse, Chris, would tell me that my mom had sparked a lengthy staff discussion about whether it was ever right to remove someone from hospice service at age 104, even if she had shown remarkable resilience. As the discussion evolved, Chris told me they realized they were dealing with what was essentially a moral question.

"We're going to find a way to keep your mom on hospice, Dave. It's what we have to do."

+

We had hospice and we had heat. But to keep my mom at home, we also needed cash. The savings I'd used to fund my mom's care had now taken us into the summer. But what next? As much as I wanted to keep my mom at home, I told myself I couldn't continue to fund her care indefinitely. And that's when I got a phone call that would alter our financial circumstances for good.

William and Susan Grindley had known my mom for nearly fifty years, and William called me with a striking proposal. The Grindleys knew I was considering moving my mom to a nursing facility and then renting the house to pay for her care. Their offer was both generous and straightforward. William said they could provide a monthly check that would cover our care costs at an interest rate lower than even a home equity loan. If

I was interested, they would draw up a simple contract securing the loan against Adelaide's house, to be repaid in full when the house was sold. He added that they were also willing to provide enough to pay off the home equity loan so that I could consolidate what was owed at the lowest possible interest rate.

William and Susan, along with their adult children, Pablo and Elena, had the resources to help. But they also loved my mom, and loved what she had done for our community. We were once again reaping the benefits of what my mom had sown.

The enduring and recurring presence of such goodwill sometimes made me wonder why we were so fortunate, why we continued to be the recipients of so much kindness. But perhaps it happens so that we ask that very question.

And my mom? She would be able to continue to live where she had for the past sixty-six years. Eileen and Sinai would still be by her side. Chris Brady and the hospice team would still visit. And I could still hold her hand in the quiet light of her bedroom. She was home, even if she no longer had central heat.

18

PICTURE FRAMES

It was now the late summer of 2016, and my mom's ability to piece together her present and her past had receded further into the misty distance. She could still say her name, especially when prompted, but she no longer remembered many of the elements of her life that she'd always carried so proudly: her Midwestern upbringing; her four sisters; the father she adored; or even my dad, the defining love of her life.

She still recognized me and responded when I told her my name. She knew I was important to her, but that was all. And that was OK. It was enough to feel like a son again.

Moments still mattered. But moments were now measured in glimpses and spoonfuls: The next face that leans over her hospital bed and smiles as her eyes shift, then focus. The next spoonful of thickened juice that she still welcomes.

And then those moments get whisked away.

By this point, my mom seemed able to access just four remaining threads of the vast tapestry that once defined her life. She knew she was Catholic. When we said a prayer together, her arms and hands still moved ever so slightly, faintly tracing the sign of the cross. She knew Stanford mattered, and that men did, too—I could tell because her eyes still lit up when either topic came up. And she knew that she was a Democrat, though the details of what that meant had faded away.

But sometimes I wondered if there wasn't still more. When I sat beside her, she still seemed so fundamentally present. When I saw those eyes flashing brightly, was she trying to tell me something more? When I saw her lean forward, rocking back and forth gently but with purpose, where was she still trying to go?

We'd continued celebrating my mom's birthdays after the big hundreth celebration, with family and friends joining us in my mom's backyard for birthdays 101 through 103. And she still loved being at the center of those gatherings.

At one of those parties, Eileen's son and a group of his friends put on a Tongan dance exhibition, injecting more life into west Menlo Park than it had witnessed in a very long time. But when we reached her 104th, it was time to honor my mom in a quieter fashion. Paul and Yoko and Eileen and I gathered around her hospital bed and sang happy birthday while holding up a cupcake with a single candle.

I found myself increasingly obsessed with wanting to remember moments like that, and to absorb all the little everyday moments, too, the ones I'd experienced with her countless times—resting my hand on hers, or always turning to look back at her each time I left the room. I used to wish I could receive an alert right before one of those iconic moments was going to take place for the last time. But now I tried to remember to just be faithful to those experiences as they unfolded. To take in each touch and each look for what it was—a singular moment where existence and time intersected and would never do so again in quite the same way.

+

One afternoon, I arrived in Menlo Park to find Eileen getting my mom ready to head outside. She was sitting in the wheelchair with her legs elevated and her coat stretched out on top. The shoulders of the coat were resting on top of my mom's stomach, with the inside of the coat facing up. I watched Eileen ease her arms into the coat sleeves and then gently pull the coat back over her head. I couldn't help but smile. My granddaughter, Hannah, and preschoolers everywhere, had learned to get their coats on the same way. Put the coat on the floor, reach in and flip it back over your head.

My granddaughter was now nearly four, my mom approaching 104. I was often struck by how life's developmental stages can sometimes intersect across time. As Hannah had acquired more sophisticated language, my mom had been losing vocabulary. One's ability to reason and communicate had leapt forward; the other's had continued to slip back. One had long since mastered using kitchen utensils; the other relied on someone else to spoon-feed her in bed. Hannah had triumphantly learned to use the bathroom the year before. My mom no longer could.

If you were to plot their lives on a graph, one's starting point would be the year 1912, the other, 2012. But now the two lines on the graph have converged and crossed. And in that intersecting geometry of development, only one arc ascends. Indeed, as Hannah's line curved ever upward, my mom's arc was closer to another intersection point—that of my six-month-old grandson, my father's namesake, William Iverson Beare.

My mom was now biting the metal spoon we used to feed her, so I bought her a plastic one instead—the same kind Laura uses to feed William. William likes to stare at his hands, fascinated by this exciting appendage, and likely imagining the mischief he'll soon make. My mom sometimes stares at her hands, too, and I find myself thinking about all her hands have accomplished these past 104 years, and all they can no longer do.

✦

The year 2016 inched along, and with it came another presidential campaign. For the first time in her life, my mom didn't know who was running. It seemed so strange that what had always been so central to her life would no longer animate her days.

My parents had always been New Deal Democrats at heart. They believed in this country and its many blessings. And they believed in flying the flag, putting one up in front of our house every Labor Day, Veteran's Day, Memorial Day, and Fourth of July. My parents believed that if you worked hard, everything would work out. It was a belief system, for my father in particular, born from weathering many challenges. His life journey—dropping out of college to support his family, and spending six years in the Army during World War II—meant he knew something about how to go through hard times. But he never lost faith in the promise of America, and he always believed in flying the flag.

It never occurred to my parents during the 1950s, '60s, and '70s that the flag represented a point of view about politics. To them, it represented a point of view about the values they lived by and the country those values stood for: hard work, decency, community service, tolerance, and opportunity.

My parents' first political hero may have been Franklin D. Roosevelt, but in the 1950s, they were fervent supporters of a Democratic presidential aspirant few people today remember: Adlai Stevenson. My mom worked hard for Stevenson's presidential campaigns in 1952, and again in 1956. When we'd complain that she was never around, she would always tell us, "We'll do more after the election."

And years later, she loved to tell the story that after Stevenson lost a second time, I complained to her with bitterness: "You spent all that time helping him, and he didn't even win."

Sometime during the 1980s, though, the flag quit flying at 1121 Westfield Dr. It wasn't because the political Right now waved the flag at every occasion, and the Left acted like they were embarrassed by it. My folks didn't fly the flag because they couldn't. My dad's Parkinson's had advanced to the point where he could no longer manage putting it up. And my mom, for all her virtues, never did anything that involved working outdoors.

But one late summer afternoon, I drove up to the house and saw a flag flapping in the breeze—an iconic reprise of all those holidays from my childhood. As I walked up, I wondered who had brought the flag back to our front porch once more.

The answer, of course, was Eileen.

"It's almost Labor Day," she said, "and it just seemed like Adelaide's house should have a flag."

Eileen's nineteen-year-old son was completing Army basic training at Ft. Sill in Oklahoma, and I knew Eileen worried about him. But she was also intensely proud of her son. A framed photograph of Private Mohammad Khan in front of the flag sits beside her bed, just as a photo of a young Captain Bill Iverson is framed on the kitchen wall.

My mom's old hero, Adlai Stevenson, would have approved.

"Patriotism," he once wrote, "is not a short and frenzied outburst of emotion, but the tranquil and steady dedication of a lifetime."

When I walked into the kitchen to see my mom on this particular day, though, she was happily looking at a different framed photograph—one our neighbor Doug Cannon had brought over from across the street. Doug had struck up a great friendship with Adelaide ever since he'd moved back into the home his parents had once occupied. And on a recent visit, he brought her a picture of his father, my parents' old friend. My mom liked it, even though she had no idea who he was—partly because he had a quality that mattered.

"He's handsome," she said.

And so we keep that picture where she can look at it in the kitchen. It makes me think she'd be just as happy with the image of any handsome young man, like the kind that often comes packaged with a picture frame when you buy it.

Does the fact that so much has gone diminish who she now is? That photo of my dad as a dashing young Army captain is framed on the wall just a few feet away. Does it matter that she no longer knows who he is? The place in her brain that once harbored a treasured memory no longer supplies the synaptic connection to say his name, but I don't think that means there's an empty space in her heart.

My parents' love still endures. It lives on in those who were nurtured by it: her three sons, her four adult grandchildren, and now four great-grandchildren. And not only does it resonate across generations, I also think it exists in ways that go beyond visual recognition. Her very core still responds to who my father was and what he represented. I think it might be what prompts her to say, "I'll take him," when I say our handsome young hospice nurse Chris is on his way. It might be what makes her eyes sparkle when our kindly priest Father Xavier arrives, opens his arms wide, and says, "Adelaide, my dear. How about a kiss?" And it might even have been what stirred inside her when she'd once looked at me and had seen a husband instead.

The love my mom and dad shared lives on because it lives in her. Recognizing love doesn't depend on recognizing a name when it can still be named by the heart. It lives on as ardently as the words my father wrote to her seventy-five years ago during the middle of WWII—words as durable as the flame that inspired them.

✦

Spring, 1942

Dear Adelaide,

I know you are an eternity away, but there is tomorrow—a long and beautiful day pressing eagerly forward for us to always clasp with gentle hands.

—Bill

✦

I believe my dad would long for another tomorrow if he were sitting by her bedside today. And I don't think he would be surprised at her presence.

"Yes," I think he'd say. "Look at you. You're still here."

The woman he once called "a beautiful hunk of flesh" might only weigh half of what she once did, and the "marvelous torso" he once described now lies curled and constricted in a hospital bed. But I think he would still recognize the "fathomless depths" of her eyes. I think he would still see *her*—a perception of the heart rather than the eyes. A perception not compromised by current circumstances. And I think he would once more long to be by her side.

Their love was impervious to time and to what it would someday subtract. Perhaps that's why, even at the age of 104, Adelaide Iverson's eyes still burned bright. She was loved in a way that stays forever kindled.

+

A month later, my mom's 2016 absentee ballot arrived. She was eight years old when women got the right to vote, and she'd voted in every presidential election for the past eighty years. It just didn't seem right that she wouldn't vote this year, even if she didn't know the candidates' names. So I decided to ask a simple question to verify her intentions.

"Mom, are you a Democrat?"

Her answer was swift and emphatic. "Absolutely!"

I held her hand, and together we marked the ballot for Hillary Rodham Clinton.

19

BETTER ANGELS

I'D NOW BECOME MORE OF AN INTIMATE WITNESS to caregiving than a provider of it, and that allowed me to reflect on the original decision that had brought me here. I had always felt that I'd chosen to take care of my mom for obvious and worthwhile reasons—she needed help and I could provide it. But having a clear rationale alone hadn't provided the renewable resource I needed to keep going. Eileen and Sinai, on the other hand, not only continued to offer exquisite care with relentless consistency, they both seemed able to sustain that effort. It was their profession, of course. But there was more to it than that—something made clear by a series of conversations I'd had with Sinai.

Sinai had long divided her time between caring for my mom and a woman named Sylvia, who was in her early nineties. One day, when I was out of town, Eileen called to tell me that Sylvia had passed away. I knew how devoted Sinai was to Sylvia, and called to offer my condolences.

Sinai described the last days of Sylvia's life with great tenderness, and then she told me something that I didn't understand: "Dave, I'm glad Sylvia died first."

I don't remember what I said exactly. Probably that I was glad she'd been there to care for Sylvia.

And then Sinai said, "Dave, I haven't told you this yet, but I'm glad I could take care of Sylvia because I'm not sure how long I would have been able to do that. I've got cancer."

I was stunned. She went on to tell me that she'd felt a lump in her breast a few months before. She hadn't told anyone, and she'd delayed seeing a doctor, but a friend had finally persuaded her to go to a clinic that provided care for low-income individuals. I realized as I listened that I'd never paid adequate attention to something as basic as where or whether Sinai received health care. And now she'd been diagnosed with stage three breast cancer, and would start chemotherapy the next week.

When I got back to town, Sinai gave me the most unusual health update I'd ever heard. She told me she was glad to experience chemo.

When I bewilderedly asked her why, she said, "It helps me understand what the people I take care of must feel like. I've always been healthy, but now I know what it feels like to have to take medicine when you don't want to. I know what it feels like to be tired and sick. It helps me understand what's going on when Adelaide says no when I'm trying to give her a pill or just help her with something. I understand what she means now, in a different way."

I don't think it would ever have occurred to me to

say what Sinai did—to be grateful for pain, or sorrow, or sickness because it helped me better understand the suffering of others. That approach, that fundamental life orientation, wasn't part of me. But it was true to her and to Eileen. And it was reaffirmed by the daily acts of caregiving they both provided.

For me, those same acts had only become more difficult as the years went by. But they seemed able to meet caregiving's incessant demands with quiet perseverance, sustained by something larger than themselves. They believed that caregiving was a true calling.

✦

Late one night, when I was sitting with Sinai at my mom's bedside, she said to me, "To do this work, you have to always do your best, even when it's 2:00 a.m. and Adelaide is asleep and no one is watching. What helps me is that I know I'm not alone with Adelaide. I know that God is with me, too."

For Eileen and Sinai, this work—caring for someone whose vulnerability is complete—was a shared enterprise. Yes, it was their profession, but it wasn't theirs alone. For them, it was also God's work. And having that additional participant seemed to give them strength for the long distance journey that caregiving inevitably becomes.

When I started taking care of my mom, I would have smiled at the idea that God was my caregiving partner, or that I'd been called to be my mom's side. And imagining how my very Catholic mom would have reacted to such a proclamation makes me smile, even now.

"Oh, come on," she would have snorted, before

returning to her cover-to-cover reading of *The New York Times.*

No, I definitely hadn't felt called to do this, but I had felt compelled. And now, as I reflected more on what prompted my choice to move in with my mom all those years before, I wondered if there was really a difference. Is feeling compelled a kind of calling?

My ten-second decision to move in with my mom had felt obvious—something that needed to be done, and I was the one who could do it. But looking back, I think there may have been another reason why I felt compelled: My mom wasn't the only person who needed help. I did, too. I just didn't know it.

My mom's needs had been obvious: help with meals and meds, help getting dressed and undressed, help in the bathroom. And perhaps more than anything, help getting to Stanford games. My needs were more hidden from view. I needed something more akin to reschooling. Because, while I was mostly a nice, mild-mannered guy, I also thought too highly of my own opinions. I needed an experience to make me less certain, less judgmental, and more accepting.

The author Anne Lamott puts it this way in her book *Traveling Mercies*: "When we are stuck in our own convictions and personas, we enter into the disease of having good ideas and being right.... We think we have a lock on truth, with our burnished surfaces and articulation, but the bigger we pump ourselves up, the easier we are to be pricked with a pin."

And I was about to get pricked. Before living with my mom, I'd never *had* to change. But there's nothing like a radical shift in scenery and circumstance to poke holes in your fundamental MO. When the person you're living with is losing her ability to reason, being excessively reasonable isn't terribly effective. Nor is the ability to analyze problems, present logical solutions, or simply be *right* sufficient for the job at hand. I needed a different kind of expert to provide the retraining necessary to contend with the uncertain new terrain where I now resided. And the person I needed was right in front of me, wielding just the right pin.

The reasons to move in with my mom had seemed straightforward at the time. But was the choice I made solely the product of my sizing up a problem and providing the logical solution? Or was there something less conscious going on that helped pull me in this new direction?

Stepping back from caregiving's daily demands gave me a chance to reconsider whether, in some deep but not unfathomable way, I had been unconsciously drawn to doing precisely what I most needed to do in life. At one level, it doesn't matter much if I didn't fully comprehend exactly why. I knew enough to do it, and you can make the argument that that's what really counts. But what if there's more to it than that? What if we are indeed drawn to the work we need to do because something else— something we can't initially even recognize—let alone name—is guiding us, compelling us to move in a new direction?

Now, of course, plenty of people, spouses in particular, take on caregiving without much choice in the matter. But my situation was different. I did have a choice. My question had become, *What compelled that decision?*

No doubt, many of us have been confronted by life choices and instinctively knew not only what we wanted to do, but what we *had* to do. A certain tipping point had taken place, and we felt an irresistible pull toward a new direction. Well, perhaps that's because there *was* an irresistible pull in that direction. Sometimes what stirs within us and compels us to move forward might only be an internal whisper, and sometimes it's more like an insight that arrives fully formed. But no matter how it arrives, what matters is how we respond to the message. Because when we pay attention to that tug, we're provided the opportunity to step forward in a new direction.

That's what I'd say happened to me when I chose to become a caregiver. I'd felt compelled to move in with my mom; I just wasn't aware of all the reasons why. And I certainly had no idea that the consequences of that decision would be so life changing or so well-aligned with my shortcomings. And that is why I no longer think I moved back into my mom's house at the age of fifty-nine simply because she needed help and I was available. That part is true, of course. But it isn't the only truth, because I needed help, too. And since I know that I didn't consciously embark on this path as an exercise in self-improvement, I'm disinclined to believe that the lessons I subsequently learned, or the gifts I received, were simply fortuitous.

I believe those insights happened because I was accompanied. They came from witnessing what true caregiving entails. The care Eileen and Sinai provided may have been guided by faith, but it was made real by their actions. Living according to one's beliefs, as author Christian Wiman observes, is finally a practical matter, "a physical act renewed (or not) at every moment."

It seems to me that the actions that matter most in life, including how we care for those we love, are physical acts that always require renewal. They are renewed (or not) by what we say and do for someone we love, whose vulnerability is complete, even when we're weary—especially when we are weary. They are renewed through persistence, both the kind Eileen and Sinai demonstrated, and the type demonstrated by my mom, the single most persistent person I've ever known.

It's the quality I saw in her daily acts of determined care during all those years with my dad. It's what she did by calling a cab and heading out into the rain to read to friends on the Stanford campus, or send them regular notes even though they lived just a few miles apart.

When my mom's best friend, Nancy Hofstadter, died, her daughter Laurie told me that she'd found mountains of Adelaide's correspondence in her mom's bedroom—letters documenting nearly sixty years of friendship, going back to their days together at Stanford Village. It's the same constancy she showed in her community work, whether it was welcoming people to the neighborhood, or registering new voters. She was renewed by action. In that sense, she was all business. But her business was us.

I don't think I would have understood that if I hadn't responded to that tug I felt in the fall of 2007. My friend Jim Neafsey, a former Jesuit, says that we both carry others in life and are carried ourselves. Sinai, Eileen, and my mom were all people who did a lot of carrying. None of them would have looked at it that way, but I think the people who do the carrying are often like that.

For Eileen and Sinai, that orientation was supported by their belief that they were being guided and supported by God. But I was never sure about how faith bolstered my mom's lifelong orientation. All she ever told me about her century-long habit of going to church was that she felt better for going. I'd never found that answer satisfying. But maybe that's all she needed to know—that she felt better and stronger for believing in something bigger than herself. As Sinai once observed, "Adelaide loved church, but she didn't talk about God. Church just reloaded her."

Maybe that's all any of us need. Maybe all that matters is our willingness to be carried beyond ourselves so that we can carry others.

I think that's why I needed to move in with my mom. I had some carrying to do, even though I didn't know it at the time. And then I wound up being carried, too. And when you experience both, it increases your capacity to persist—both in the work you choose to create, and in the love you choose to cherish. I don't think any of that happened by coincidence.

✦

Where did all this reflection leave me? Where would I turn next if I ever needed to try to go the distance for someone else I loved?

The idea of turning to church and God for strength was something I'd resisted most of my adult life. And to reconsider that possibility prompted the same kind of reluctance in me that Anne Lamott wrote about when describing her own faith dilemma, in *Traveling Mercies:* "It seemed an utterly impossible thing that simply could not be allowed to happen.... But then everywhere I went, I had the feeling that a little cat was following me, wanting me to reach down and pick it up, wanting me to open the door and let it in. But I knew what would happen: you let a cat in one time, you give it a little milk, and then it stays forever."

But having had a little space, both literally and figuratively, to further reflect on the question of faith, I've decided it's OK to put the milk out. And that's because I had learned that providing sustaining care can't be a solo project. My mom, Sinai, Eileen, and I all carried each other, and sometimes that takes heavy lifting. We don't just need what Lincoln called the better angels of our nature; we need to sustain and feed them. We need an accompanying faith that's powered by everyday acts of kindness—a faith that propels and reinforces our service to others in this hard, gritty, fragile, and beautiful world. Whether that's called having faith in God, or simply having faith in the possibility of human goodness, I'm not sure matters very much. All I know is that we're not alone—that we are restored when we act in common, according to the tenets of the heart. And when we have a faith that propels us outward, we are replenished by the gifts we receive and the gifts we provide.

That's why I'm OK with putting the saucer out. I know I'll always need replenishment—a lap of faith, not necessarily a leap.

20

LIFE SUPPORT REDUX

IT WAS NOW OCTOBER 2016, and time seemed to accelerate as the pace of my mom's physical deterioration quickened. It hadn't been that long since she could wave to people as we walked down the street, announcing her presence and eliciting a response—still able to physically engage with her own unfolding story. But by October, she'd been on hospice a full year; way beyond the usual norm. She was continuing to lose weight, her voice was softer, and her words were often slurred. It had begun to feel like, despite her iron will, her vise-like grip on life might be slipping away.

✦

> One thing that's clearer to
> me now is the unforeseen
> consequence of wonderful care:
> continued life. Sometimes I
> wonder if providing that is always
> the right thing to do. But how
> can I not?

Sometimes I try to put myself
in Adelaide's place and imagine
what she wants. And I think she
wants to be cared for. I think
she wants to be warm and dry,
to be nurtured with softened
food and the thickened drink
she can still swallow. I think she
wants to know she still matters.
She wouldn't get all that at a
nursing home. She would get less
attention, less care, less warmth.
She'd be wetter and more alone.
It's that basic. She can't tell me
what she wants. But I think I
know.

—October 2016

As November approached, I felt the time had come
to talk with our hospice nurse, Chris Brady, about how
we would treat my mom if she got pneumonia again or
another urinary tract infection. I was ready to decline
antibiotic treatment so long as we could keep her
comfortable, but I wasn't sure whether Eileen would feel
the same way.

Eileen loved Adelaide with fierce devotion. She was
the organizing principle in both our lives, but only one of
us would have been truly happy to have that orientation
sustained. To make a decision that might shorten my
mom's life would carry a different consequence for her

than it would for me, or Sinai, or anyone in the family.

I told Eileen my feelings about declining future antibiotics, and I was relieved that she agreed.

"It's OK," she said. "It's time."

Before conveying this to Chris, I also checked in with the immediate family, and everyone was in accord. But there was someone else whose opinion I wasn't completely sure about—my mom. There was the Adelaide who'd authoritatively signed an advanced directive at age ninety-seven—the Adelaide who'd always approached these questions with steely certainty. And there was the present Adelaide, who still clung fiercely to life.

I wanted to be true to the core of who she had always been, while still honoring her current tenacity. I wanted to be true to her life story, but I also knew that inevitably, that truth would be filtered through my own perceptions, and perhaps my own priorities. But I also believed that I understood her, just as she understood me. And even more than that, my mom had always believed in me, which is the greatest gift any parent can give. I felt that she would trust me to make this decision. And for that reason, as much as any, I felt clarity rather than confusion about our decision not to treat a future UTI.

Chris always began his nursing visits the same way—by greeting my mom with warmth and unfailing politeness.

"How are you, Mrs. Iverson?"

His careful exam included taking her vital signs, and he would ask her permission before checking her temperature or blood pressure, explaining clearly and respectfully what he was going to do. When he was finished, we'd always follow the same protocol. Rather than talk about her in the third person while standing next to her bed, we'd all leave the room to have our follow-up conversation.

On this particular day, Chris observed that he thought something had shifted in Adelaide's overall condition. I told him what we'd decided about antibiotics, and he nodded in quiet agreement. He understood.

But that didn't end our discussion. Chris brought up other circumstances we might face. What if my mom got a bedsore? Would we accept antibiotics in that instance? I knew right away that I would, perhaps because bedsores can be so painful. Eileen, who was always part of these conversations, felt the same way. What if her blood oxygen level drops, and providing her with oxygen via portable tank and nasal tube would make her breathing less stressful? Would we be OK with that?

I was fine with that option, as was Eileen.

So why did some life-support treatments feel appropriate, and others not? As we talked it through, the concept that would guide our decision-making became clearer: to provide comfort without prolonging life unduly. Giving her extra oxygen through a non-invasive nasal tube would keep her comfortable if her breathing became more labored, but it wouldn't cure anything or prolong her life in a consequential way. Treating a bedsore with an antibiotic ointment would be curative, but its primary function was comfort, not life extension. With a UTI, on the other hand, antibiotic treatment could extend life for many months, and Chris was confident that the discomfort could be managed by other means.

Were we straining to meet some hypothetical standard of consistency? Perhaps. But what felt right was to let my mom's comfort guide the choices we might soon face. It wouldn't be a guaranteed, fail-safe approach, but at least it was a standard that could help us sift through the granular details that inevitably accompany the end of life.

And then Chris said, "You're not thinking of taking any other steps, are you?"

Without saying anything further, I thought I knew where he might be headed. Swallowing was more difficult for my mom now. She only consumed occasional puréed vegetables, plus thickened juice or water, supplemented with Ensure. It would be possible to keep her comfortable just by giving her thickened juice, but that didn't feel right. My mom had always enjoyed food, and it was clear she still did. Even though, by most definitions, it didn't seem like real food.

"We want to keep giving her the sustenance she wants," I said to Chris.

He nodded in agreement and then told us that he was confident we could keep my mom calm and less anxious by using pain and anti-anxiety medication.

We all felt her time might be short, and we all knew we might be wrong. But we had our plan, and we would see what would happen next.

✦

Over the next month, my mom continued to decline. October became November 2016. It had now been nine years since I'd moved in with my mom, and eight months since I'd moved out. She still took in nourishment, but she was cloudier, less able to speak. Eileen suspected that she might have another UTI, and Chris thought that was likely, too. We decided there was no point in taking a urine sample, given the decision we'd made.

But what was once abstract was now real. I'd felt clear and calm when deciding to withhold antibiotics, but now that likely reality was here.

I stood beside my mom's bed and looked at her, a curled shadow of her former self. I didn't have second thoughts, but a second round of what-ifs set in. What if we weren't able to keep her comfortable? What if this went on and on?

+

If my mom could have articulated how she viewed death at that point, I think she still would have aligned herself with the scientist Steven Jay Gould, who published a famous essay on this subject in 1985. Gould was facing an aggressive form of cancer where the median life expectancy was less than a year. His essay was titled "The Median isn't the Message," and in its most quoted passage, Gould referenced the words of the poet Dylan Thomas: "It has become, in my view, a bit too trendy to regard the acceptance of death as something tantamount to intrinsic dignity.... For most situations, however, I prefer the more martial view that death is the ultimate enemy—and I find nothing reproachable in those who rage mightily against the dying of the light."

Gould was only forty-four years old when he wrote that essay, and his refusal to accept the median life expectancy for his diagnosis made sense. Indeed, he went on to live another eighteen years. But what does it mean to actively resist the dying of the light at age 104?

My mom didn't actually rage. Her resistance was more like an insistent perseverance. And the intensity of her feelings still seemed evident, especially if you believed her eyes. For that reason, I think how we define a "good death" depends entirely on point of view and timing. That is, whether you're contemplating your own death or someone else's, and whether you're looking out into the future or you're at death's door.

When I thought about my mom's death, I knew I longed for what might not be likely. I hoped that when that moment came, and we'd all had a chance to take her into our hearts, that she would draw a gentle last breath and be at peace. That's what I longed for. But I wasn't my mom, and I knew she would probably want to be in motion until the moment her shoulders settled and her body finally grew still. Being at peace was never part of her life's lexicon.

In the coming weeks, my mom continued to hang on, reminding me again of everyone's favorite *Adelaide as a force of nature* comparison. Even now, lying contracted in her hospital bed, weighing no more than eighty pounds, she still radiated a certain firepower. We could all feel it. It's what propels the question she'll still ask while lying in her hospital bed.

"What are we going to do now?" she'll say, and then kick at the guardrail to show that she's ready.

When you were in the room with her, there was no question who was at its center. We talked to her and she radiated back—a conversation that was felt as much as heard.

Christian Wiman has written about the communication that takes place even as our cellular makeup begins to disintegrate.

"If quantum entanglement is true, if related particles react in similar or opposite ways even when separated by tremendous distance, then it is obvious that the whole world is alive and communicating in ways we do not fully understand. And we are part of that life, part of that communication—even as, maybe even especially as—our atoms begin the long dispersal we call death."

Perhaps my mom has already begun to shed the atoms that compose her body. But those atoms were still ricocheting around us, and my bet was that they would continue to do so, long after she was gone.

+

Adelaide: I'm afraid.

Me: What are you afraid of, Mom?

Adelaide: Never. I'm never.

Me: You're afraid of never?

Adelaide: Yes.

Me: You're afraid of never what?

Adelaide: I'm afraid of never getting out of here. I can't help them.

—November 2016

+

I thought about that interchange often. What did she mean when she said, "I'm afraid of never getting out of here?" Could she mean that she was finally ready to leave life behind, and was afraid she'd keep on living?

I couldn't persuade myself into believing that was true. I think it's more likely that she was afraid she wouldn't be able to get out of her present situation—the trap her body and hospital bed had become. I think she was afraid she wouldn't ever again be part of the action. And that's why the last words are the most important: "I can't help them."

If she couldn't get out of that damn hospital bed, she couldn't help whoever needed her. And why be accepting of that?

I think my mom resisted death because of what might still be possible. To her, that meant death should be approached with a spirit of combat rather than calm. But it still worried me. I didn't want her to die afraid.

As Christian Wiman remarks, a good death is, to some extent, a matter of good fortune and timing. In reflecting on his grandmother's life of gentle service, a life that ended in the throes of great stress and fear, Wiman writes, "I must believe in the scope and momentum of her life, not the awful and anomalous instant of her death."

So, too, with my mom. What should matter most is the long, continuous arc of a life that will always reverberate. She was never about stasis. It is one more lesson from her restive life: don't take a day off, not even when you're 104.

She was lasting evidence of Newton's first law of physics: a body in motion tends to stay in motion, even if it is only to rock back and forth or stretch out a leg in hopes of taking one more step.

Perhaps what I should yearn for, is that when death approaches, she leans forward with eyes burning bright, and says one last time, "What are we going to do now?"

And then her atoms would still do the walking.

21

WINTER STARS

MY MOM WAS STILL WITH US as we approached the holiday season once more. And now, an additional crossroads moment was front and center in my emotional life: Lynn and I had decided to get married.

We'd been together for eighteen years, but we hadn't lived under the same roof until the last eight months. For reasons we usually avoided articulating, we had never talked much about the M-word. We maintained a careful togetherness, coupled with intentional independence, and my decision to take care of my mom had not exactly enhanced relationship growth.

"We're fully committed to each other," we'd say. "But we can't really think about living together or getting married until after Adelaide is gone."

Looking back, we both think that either by way of avoidance, or intention, we placed our relationship on extended hold—one full stop short of true commitment. So it wasn't a coincidence that our decision to take the last big step in our relationship happened after I'd finally stepped away from my day-to-day caregiving responsibilities.

My mom was still present in both our lives, but she was no longer my primary point of orientation. And beyond that, the current reality that my mom might soon die made it feel important that we not delay any further. Perhaps we both sensed, without ever acknowledging it, that waiting to get married until after her death was extending a delaying tactic we'd indulged in for too long. One conversation led to another, obstacles fell away, and motivation fell in place. At age sixty-eight, we were getting married.

Marriage obviously occupied a different place along life's continuum than my mom's mortality. But the two were more connected than not. Perhaps that's because there's a certain fullness that all of life's deepest experiences share: The birth of a grandchild, or the death of a grandparent. The moment a marriage begins, or the moment a spouse of many decades passes on. Moments etched into our core that clarify life's beauty and its tender frailty.

I thought about my mom the day Lynn and I got married—what she would make of it, and if she had been able to attend, what kind of comment she might have volunteered in the middle of the ceremony.

+

Our lovely late-November wedding was held at our closest friends' home in the Oakland hills. My older brother, Peter, wasn't able to travel, so he and his wife, Kaaren, couldn't come. But Paul and Yoko were there, as were my daughter, Laura, and my son-in-law, Kevin, my two nieces, Lynn's three adult children, her extended family, and our closest friends. And Eileen and Sinai were there, having arranged for a friend to stay with Adelaide. I remember looking out at them as our small wedding ceremony began, feeling how right it was that they could witness this new chapter in our family journey.

+

Christmas was approaching, and in the Christian tradition, the Advent season is a time of watchfulness. We are to be alert for what may lie ahead. And as Christmas grew near, we all watched as my mom slowly grew stronger once more. Whether it had actually been another UTI, or some other foe, she had once again swatted away whatever was trying to lay her low—this time, without the benefit of antibiotics. She grew more communicative, able to say a few sentences, able to smile. She was more alert and responsive. She looked pretty great, actually. It made me smile, shake my head, and sigh all at the same time. Which is life, pretty much.

She would be here for one more Christmas.

The last time I'd visited the house, Eileen told me that she'd played holiday songs for Adelaide the night before and danced by her bedside.

And then she added, with a grin, "Adelaide tried to raise her arms and snap her fingers."

I smiled, but I couldn't quite share in her enthusiasm.

When Sinai arrived with a Christmas orchid—something she'd done for many Christmases past—I thanked her, and she replied, "No, Dave. Thank you."

She went on to tell me how grateful she was for all that Adelaide and I had made possible, and how much she appreciated being part of our family. I felt small as she told me this.

Eileen and Sinai, I thought. *Eileen and Sinai.*

A few nights later, I pulled up to the house once more. It looked as it always did at Christmastime: The tree was placed in front of the living-room window, shining brightly for all to see, just as one had for sixty-six Christmases before. When I walked in, the inside of the house was decorated as always, too, with our old family Christmas cards still hanging where we'd placed them during Christmas in October fourteen months before. The cards spanned the years my mom had spent in that home, from the black and white photos of us gathered around the fireplace, to a last series of cards from recent years—ones featuring my mom holding up her autographed Stanford football, another from her hundredth birthday celebration, and another that featured her four grandchildren. Seeing the last one made me smile.

A few weeks before, Paul and Yoko's daughter, Ayuko, and her boyfriend, Ajith, had visited Adelaide. As they were leaving the house, Ajith turned to Ayuko and asked her to wait in the car for a moment because he'd left something behind in Adelaide's room. But he actually had other intentions.

Ajith went back to Adelaide's bedroom and leaned over to ask her a question.

"Grandma Adelaide. I want you to know that I'd like to ask Ayuko to marry me. But before I do, I'd like your permission."

Her voice was soft, but her answer couldn't have been more clear.

"OK."

I paused for a moment to look around at the living room and take in that familiar scene once more. I will always associate this old house with Christmas, I thought. We all will.

And someday soon, we'd have Ajith and Ayuko's card to add to the family collection.

I knew I would always hold that image of my mom's house at Christmastime close to my heart. But it was also a little different to come back now that I no longer lived here. Even though I talked to Eileen or Sinai nearly every day, I didn't know all the details from the past forty-eight or seventy-two hours—the ups and downs, how much my mom had slept that afternoon, or how much thickened juice she'd consumed. I knew the essentials, but not the ebb and flow, the rhythms of her day.

But when I walked into my mom's bedroom, I knew right away that on this December night, she was in a different place. There wasn't any restlessness. She just seemed quiet and calm. She looked to be—remarkably—at peace.

We just sat there for a long time, holding hands, and I felt a wave of tenderness come over me

After a while, my mom looked at me, and said in a voice that was soft and only slightly slurred, "You look wonderful."

I told her she did, too. "We make a good pair."

She smiled. "What a pair."

We sat for a while, my hand on top of hers, just sitting together, nothing more.

And then she turned her head to me. "I feel lucky."

She said it with more clarity than anything I'd heard her say in recent months.

I told her that I felt lucky, too. Lucky for all that she'd added to my life and to the lives of those around her, and that I would always remember what she'd taught me.

And then she said it again: "I feel lucky."

So I asked her if she could tell me why.

There was a long pause, and then she looked at me with eyes as bright as winter stars and said:

"Because there is love all around."

There had been plenty of times in recent years when I hadn't felt that love was all around, or even felt that love was around at all. But in that moment, I knew she was right. That even in difficult times—perhaps, especially in difficult times—unexpected love can still be found. You just have to be lucky enough to reach out and discover a welcoming embrace in return.

Now, that embrace encircled me. It came from my new wife Lynn, from Sinai and Eileen, and it came, of course, from my mom. My time as a caregiver had both drained me and filled me up, encompassing some of the hardest moments in my life and some of the most beautiful. I got both, and that had made all the difference.

On that Christmas night, I felt something I hadn't experienced before. That while my time with my mom was still unfinished, our journey was now complete. We had endured our bursts of anger and frustration, but over time, our deep and abiding connection had always held.

We were both less wed to our own sense of certainty. I wanted that to be true, anyway, and I sensed my mom did, too.

We had found a steadying. And while the currents of time and age had taken us into territory we'd never imagined, we'd kept traveling, and that journey had carried us to our truest destination as mother and son. It had brought me to the bedside of someone I loved so that I could hear the deepest of all truths: that love is all around.

22

LAST CALL

THE CALL CAME ONE YEAR TO THE DAY after my mom and I had that conversation. It was 11:30 at night on Saturday, December 16, 2017.

"David," Eileen says. "Adelaide isn't doing well. She's not herself. Would you call hospice?"

She tells me that Adelaide isn't responsive and hadn't been answering her questions. I tell her that I'll call hospice and ask for a nurse to come out right away.

And then I say, "Do you want me to come?"

With no hesitation, she says "Yes. Come."

As I hurry to get ready to go, I think about how my mom had seemed weaker in recent days. Just forty-eight hours earlier, when I'd last been there, Eileen and I had mused about whether something was once again shifting. The week before, our hospice nurse Chris had detected a small amount of fluid in my mom's lungs, but that was something he'd detected before, and she had always brushed it off like a runny nose.

But then yesterday, Chris had called to tell me he'd detected more fluid in her lungs, and that her blood oxygen level, which had always been a perfect 99 percent, had dropped to near 90 percent. He'd decided to start her on oxygen, just to keep her more comfortable. Chris knew my mom extremely well, and he sounded different on the phone. Perhaps we really were at a turning point.

We said goodbye. And then after we hung up, I swung back in the other direction. This was Adelaide Iverson, and she always came back.

Now, Eileen is telling me to come.

I call hospice, and they tell me a nurse will be there within the hour. I finish throwing a few things into an overnight bag, give Lynn a kiss, and head out the door.

There is something comforting about late-night drives, even in the perpetually restless Bay Area. The intrusive glare of daytime distractions is less present. The relentless traffic grows more muted. There's less static. Your thoughts can drift, conjuring up images that float back and envelop you.

I speed south on I-880, past a brightly lit solitary Ferris wheel still rotating through the night. I think about the long arc of my mom's remarkable life, and whether we were about to arrive at the end of her journey. I imagine her now in her bedroom of sixty-seven years. Only, now she lies in a hospital bed, tiny and tethered to an oxygen tank. And I also know that she is not alone—that Eileen is sitting nearby, keeping watch. It is Advent once more.

I drive on, full of wonder. Is my mom wondering, too? Or is she beyond wonder?

I drive on through the quiet night, approaching my

childhood home, feeling both alone and accompanied, filled with an aching sadness—but filled, nonetheless.

✦

When I get to Menlo, the on-duty nurse is already there and has almost finished checking my mom. She and Eileen and I then step out into the hallway, and with a kind and gentle manner, the nurse begins her explanation. Even with added oxygen, she tells us, Adelaide's blood oxygen level has continued to drop. Adelaide is also breathing more rapidly—about thirty breaths a minute, or double the normal rate—so the nurse had given her a small dose of morphine to help her relax and slow her breathing.

"It will help keep her more comfortable," she says.

I ask what everyone always asks in this situation: "I know it's impossible to predict, but do you think this means she's approaching the end?"

The nurse gives me a gentle smile. "I've looked at your mom's chart, and I know she's been extraordinary. But yes, I think she doesn't have lots more time. I don't think anything is imminent, but I do think it's a matter of days. A week at most."

Eileen and I both nod and look down. And then we say goodbye.

We go back to my mom's room and sit with her at her bedside. It's quiet, and dark, and cold, and peaceful. At 2:00 a.m., I stretch out on the living room couch for a few hours while Eileen maintains her vigil. And so began what would become our routine for the days ahead. We would alternate. We would keep watch.

Throughout the next day, she seems to just be resting.

She's no longer alert, no longer talking. No longer taking in food or drink. But her breathing is back to a normal rate, and her blood oxygen level is back to 98 percent.

I ask Eileen if she thought it would be OK if I drove home to Oakland for a few hours and returned later in the evening. Lynn and I were hosting a neighborhood Christmas party.

"Yes," she says, "That will be fine. Adelaide is doing OK."

+

When I return later that evening, my mom is awake but it isn't clear what she takes in. The eyes that always burned bright are filmier now and only partly open. She leans slightly forward, her head bobbing gently back and forth, like a stricken bird softly probing the air around her. I wonder if she's trying to determine where she is, or even who she is.

I tell her that we're here. We're with her. We will always be with her. She makes soft, cheeping sounds and gurgles gently.

She is so very small, almost skeletal, with skin stretched across the bones of her face. Her head and shoulders continue their rhythmic rocking. She no longer seems fully conscious, yet as ever, her body yearns to be in motion, as if still eager to take flight. Is this some kind of ultimate muscle memory? That even as life ebbs, the core of who she is still propels her forward? Or is what animates her not merely physical? Perhaps what still pulls her forward is a remaining seedling of her deep religious faith—that fundamental teaching that leading a good life means being in motion for the benefit of others. That you only reap what you sow, a journey that never ceases.

With each breath, with each expansion of her chest, perhaps she is bringing herself, and us, closer to the interconnected pulse of humankind.

And then her head returns to the pillow and she rests.

✦

Once more, we keep watch through the night. Breaths are OK. Blood oxygen is OK.

I ask Eileen, "If you were to describe Adelaide to someone who never knew her, what would you say?"

"She's a ball of fire," Eileen says. "She burns so bright."

I think about how we're drawn to her in the same way we're always drawn to fire. She has an energy that keeps pulling people together without ever burning out. I think about how fire exudes warmth and light, but that it also provides spark and the prospect of fearsome power. And as Eileen and I both know, she could be fearsome. When she was unhappy with you, she'd just glare. Every once in a while, I'd try to glare back, but it never worked out very well.

✦

Eileen tells me that she hadn't wanted to observe her prayer ritual this morning. Her phone is programmed to deliver the traditional morning call to prayer, but she says that this morning, she wanted to ignore it. Then she thought about Adelaide, and that made her want to pray.

"Adelaide keeps my faith strong," she says.

Eileen tells me that she asked Allah what would happen to her when Adelaide was gone. And she said the answer that came back to her was, "Don't you worry about what you'll do. Allah will take care of that. Your job is to worry about Adelaide."

It's now early morning, thirty hours after I received Eileen's call, and it's still dark outside. The house is cold, but my mom's room isn't. The space heaters are still doing their job. I smile with the thought that my mom did indeed make it into yet another winter, and there's still no central heat.

Eileen and I both say we're not sad. We talk about how joy exists within sorrow, fullness within loss. I think we both feel enriched by this life before us—Adelaide's life, a force that always propelled her forward, pulling all of us forward. Now, that forward motion is growing more still, and yet she still exerts a gravitational pull.

My mom hasn't spoken since I arrived, so I ask Eileen about the last time she heard her speak. She says it happened the same day that she called me. And then Eileen tells me about the last conversation she had with my mom, and the last words she would likely ever speak.

"I was sitting with her, and she looked up and said, 'I want to go.' And I wondered if that meant she was finally ready to leave this life. So I said to her, 'Well, where do you want to go, Adelaide?' And Adelaide looked at me and said, 'Downtown.'"

Later that morning, Sinai arrives. She talks about her ongoing breast cancer treatment, and how being with Adelaide has helped keep her strong.

"This is what I learned from Adelaide," she says. "You have to be positive. No matter what. There are no excuses. You have to keep going. You have to help others."

Like Eileen, she tells me that being with Adelaide has strengthened her understanding of what having faith really means. I ask her how, and she tells me this story:

"One day, we were sitting in the kitchen and Adelaide says to me, 'Sinai, how are you going to make the world a better place?' I thought about it for a while, and then I said, 'I'm just going to pick one person or one family to help.' Adelaide put down the paper and looked at me and said, 'That's good. I think you're right.'"

Monday drifts along. Chris comes by for another visit. We don't talk much. We don't need to. I call Father Xavier, the pastor for the Catholic Community at Stanford, who'd been a faithful visitor in recent years. I ask him if he can visit once more.

"Of course," he says.

And then my lapsed Catholic nature betrays me. "Will you give her last rites?"

He pauses and then responds gently. "Well, we haven't called it that for a long time. It's now the Anointing of the Sick, and I've anointed your mom many times." And then he chuckles. "In fact, she's so well-oiled, she's going to slip right into heaven."

Monday becomes Tuesday. The day drifts on. Eileen and I sit with her, watching, and talk quietly. Sinai won't be back until Wednesday. She's going through another round of chemo and is scheduled for a treatment today. She's not even half as old as my mom. She says she'll come by after she's done at the hospital.

Eileen scolds her. "Don't you come, my sister. You go home and rest."

My mom hasn't taken in any drink or sustenance in the last forty-eight hours. Eileen says she likely won't again. Nor has she said anything, and I wonder if that ever-persistent voice really has been stilled.

Around midnight, I stretch out for a few hours on the living room sofa. At 1:30 a.m., Eileen wakes me.

"David," she whispers. "You better come."

I rise quickly and head for the bedroom. She isn't breathing. I watch for ten or fifteen seconds, not believing what I'm seeing.

"Is she gone?" I whisper, and feel a flash of anger. "Why didn't you wake me sooner?"

Eileen just keeps looking at Adelaide. And then my mom breathes again.

"She's here, David," Eileen says. "She's here."

Her breathing returns, but it's slow and irregular. I'm not sure what to do. Eileen, my constant companion and guide, isn't sure either. Do we keep the oxygen tube in place? Does it matter? Is she uncomfortable? Do we give her more morphine to ease any distress?

At 2:30 a.m., I call hospice. I'm on hold for fifteen minutes and finally hang up. Ten minutes later, I try again, and again I'm placed on hold. But after a few minutes, a duty nurse comes on the line. I describe what's happening and ask what we should do.

"We're here to support you," she says. "We want you to do what you feel is right. What you feel comfortable doing."

Exasperated, I snap, "That's not exactly helpful," and hang up.

It's 3:00 a.m. Adelaide is grimacing. And she is

someone who almost never showed any indication that she experienced pain.

We decide to give her a drop of morphine. It seems to help. But a half-hour later, she seems distressed again. I call hospice once more and ask that they send a nurse to the house.

"I think my mom is dying. Please have someone come."

At 4:00 a.m., an on-call nurse calls back and says she's an hour away but will get there as soon as she can.

The early morning wears on. She's restless. Her breaths are short and shallow and irregular. I count six breaths in a minute. Then ten a minute. Then fifteen. Then six again. We administer another drop of morphine and wait. It's 5:15 a.m., and no sign of the hospice nurse. Eileen and I don't talk much. We just watch.

＋

It's now 6:00 a.m. I find myself getting irritated all over again. Where in the world is the nurse? I call hospice again. At 6:30, the nurse calls back from her car.

"Sorry," she says. "The traffic has been bad. But when I get there, I can help you."

An hour later, she finally arrives.

"What in the world took so long?" Without waiting for a response, I lead her silently back to the room.

She listens to Adelaide's chest, and I ask her what we should do. She suggests that we talk in the other room.

The nurse tells us that we should feel free to give her morphine, as needed.

"Morphine is your friend," she says.

I find this irritating.

"Now is a time for you to cherish your mother and to be with her."

I find this hugely irritating.

"I think we know that," I say, my voice cold.

"I can stay as long as you'd like me to," she replies. "I can stay here until the end comes."

"That won't be necessary." I head back to my mom's room without saying goodbye.

✦

I stew in my irritation. I had often wondered what this last time with my mom would be like—this crossroads where life and love and death all intersect. What I'd feel and say. And here I am, just getting annoyed.

I'd been sending out periodic texts to family—my brothers, my daughter, and my mom's three other grandchildren. But now I give them each a call and let them know where things stand.

Our hospice nurse, Chris, is back on duty and comes by the house mid-morning.

"I don't think it will be long, Dave. A few hours, perhaps. Not much more." He removes my mom's oxygen tube. "She doesn't really need this anymore."

My brother Paul and his wife, Yoko, arrive. Our former caregiver Roanet arrives, too. She still works at Stanford Hospital, and her mural depicting Adelaide's life still adorns the dining room wall.

She talks gently to Adelaide. "I have a new boyfriend. You'd like him. He's Irish."

My mom's breaths are slower now—just four to six a minute. Eileen is out in the kitchen. I leave for a minute, then come back. I look at my mom. She isn't breathing.

Thirty seconds pass. I ask Roanet if she took a breath while I was gone.

"Just as you came back," she says.

I watch her. She doesn't breathe.

"Go get Eileen," I say.

Eileen comes in and looks at Adelaide. She smiles and looks at me.

"You can call the hospice nurse, David. She's gone."

"Are you sure?"

"Yes," she says. "Yes."

+

Months earlier, Eileen and I had talked about this moment, and she had a request.

"After Adelaide's gone, let's not call the mortuary right away. We'll have to call hospice to certify her death, but we don't have to call for the hearse. I think we should have some time with her. I want to prepare her properly."

Three years prior, Eileen had made a pilgrimage of sorts to India. Though she was born in Fiji, her father was of Indian descent, and going to India had always been one of her dreams. While she was there, she ordered a special outfit for Adelaide—a lavender tunic and white muslin pants. The pants had to be specially made, Eileen told me, in order to have pockets. She knew Adelaide couldn't abide pants that didn't have pockets, and Eileen wanted to make sure they were just right.

I didn't realize it at the time, but Eileen wanted Adelaide to wear that special outfit after she died. When she told me its purpose later, I smiled and asked her if she'd ever told my mom.

"Oh yes," she said. "Adelaide loves it. You know, that

tunic is her favorite color."

And she did love that tunic and pants. From time to time, she'd ask Eileen to go get her "special outfit" so that she could admire it. As I think back on it, it strikes me that she was completely comfortable with admiring the outfit she'd wear after her death, yet never comfortable with the thought of dying. Or at least, I don't think she was. Right up until the time when she could no longer communicate clearly, she'd said, "I don't want to die." And yet she grinned like a teenager, contemplating her lavender tunic. Maybe it was simply that she always wanted to look good. And Eileen, Roanet, and Sinai are now going to make sure that she does.

I leave the room to call the family while Roanet and Eileen change the sheets and gently cleanse Adelaide. I call Sinai, who'd just gotten done with chemo.

"I'm on my way," she says.

As I head back to the room, Roanet tells me she has to leave for work. I tell her how much we'd always loved having her there. That her bright smile, colorful paintings, and perpetual willingness to take my mom on long drives had been a godsend.

She smiles. "It was always my honor to help Adelaide. And it's my honor to be here today."

+

A short while later, Sinai arrives and heads straight for Adelaide's room. She takes over for Eileen, who'd been holding Adelaide's jaw in place so that it wouldn't droop. Sinai would keep her gentle grip on Adelaide for another half-hour, until she was sure Adelaide would look the way she would have wanted.

I call a few friends and neighbors to see if they want to stop by. Father Xavier comes by, too, white robed and exuding warmth, as always. Everyone looks at Adelaide and smiles with admiration. She would have liked that.

Lynn arrives with dinner, thinking there'd only be a few of us. But somehow her curry dinner becomes like the loaves and fish, and feeds us all. She asks if there was anything I'd like.

"Scotch," I reply.

It's now the evening of December 20th, the day before the winter solstice, so darkness comes quickly. But my mom's room is bright and warm. And she, as always, is at its center.

We eat, and laugh, and talk, and tell stories. Another hour passes, and I realize that Lynn isn't back. I text her. No response. But we keep talking, keep telling stories.

And then I hear the front door open.

I walk out to the hallway and say to Lynn, with another flash of irritation, "Where were you? It's our last time with Adelaide."

She nods and holds out a bottle of scotch.

＋

It has been five hours since my mom's death, and the mortuary hearse will be coming in another half-hour. We gather around her bed and each say a few words about who she'd been to us and who she'd always be.

Sinai sums up Adelaide like this: "There are people who die with all their goodness still inside them. They didn't share it. But Adelaide emptied out her goodness. She left it to everyone she was leaving behind. When she passed, she'd emptied herself out."

Only later would it occur to me that Sinai had described what should have been listed as her cause of death: she'd finally emptied herself out.

We pass around a box of chocolates that someone brought, probably knowing that Adelaide had always loved them. And suddenly, I know what those pants pockets are for. I slip a piece of chocolate into her front right pocket and kiss her forehead. Her skin is cold, but she looks like a million bucks.

Eileen and Sinai had made up Adelaide's bed in her favorite sheets—soft white, with a lavender flower pattern. Eileen had told me earlier in the day that Adelaide was not going to just be slid onto the gurney without being properly protected. So when the hearse arrives and the doorbell rings, Eileen and Sinai begin to tend to her body for the final time.

With the utmost care and compassion, and with the precision that comes when love and skill are honed by experience, Eileen and Sinai begin to carefully wrap her body in those lovely, soft sheets. I watch as they nestle first the fitted sheet, and then the top sheet, around her. They do it with the same stately ritual as the uniformed soldiers who fold the flag that covers the coffin at a military funeral.

And then Eileen says, "I'm sorry, Adelaide. But now I have to cover your beautiful face."

They lift her onto the gurney, and we wheel Adelaide out into the cold December night.

It was the kind of night my mom had always loved. Perhaps she and my dad had shared such a night when they first moved into the house at 1121 Westfield Drive, in

December 1950—a night bright with winter stars and the promise of all those tomorrows.

My mom is lifted into the back of the hearse, and then the low black car crawls away, rounding the curve of the street that Adelaide had always loved, and gliding into the darkness beyond.

EPILOGUE

FOUR MONTHS AFTER MY MOM DIED, Lynn went in for her regular mammogram. The technicians didn't like what they saw, and a subsequent MRI showed a substantial mass. A biopsy followed, revealing an aggressive form of breast cancer called Triple Negative. The tumor was large, and the cancer had already advanced into her lymph nodes. It was stage three.

In the long weeks that followed, I told myself that despite the scary statistics associated with Lynn's diagnosis, we were lucky. We were lucky to be otherwise fit and strong. Lucky to have the stability of a loving relationship, and the support of our mutual families. And we were profoundly lucky to have the resources to get good care.

I believed all of that, most of the time. I believed it, in part, because Lynn has the ability to view each day, and life in general, as an opportunity for light rather than dark. For Lynn, a day when the glass is half-full is a bad day. There's a tendency to think that people who have that orientation were just born with a sunny-side-up approach to life, blissfully immune to the contrary evidence the world offers each day. But I don't think that's giving them their due. I think having that mindset requires making certain choices each day.

It's the same attitude I saw my mom deploy when dealing with my dad's Parkinson's, and in her own resolute approach to aging. It's a perspective that requires maintaining visceral practicality—that whatever has happened, you're ready to tackle what comes next.

Lynn has maintained that outlook throughout her cancer treatment, and I've tried hard to do the same. To bring a full heart to the journey ahead. To be both tender and strong. It means always aiming toward hope. It means taking in the replenishment I need. I keep putting the saucer out, and it keeps being refilled.

The sustenance comes from our friends and family. It comes from Eileen and Sinai, who both check in with us regularly. Lynn and Sinai smile about the sisterhood of cancer treatment, and Sinai's ongoing recovery has given Lynn added strength and inspiration.

Later that summer, as Lynn's chemotherapy treatment progressed, I decided there was something else I wanted to do: I wanted to run in one more New York City marathon. And this time, my daughter Laura joined me. She was approaching forty, and I had just turned seventy. Our motto was 70 + 40 = 26.2.

We made it to the finish line. And Lynn, and our extended family, were there to cheer us on.

✦

So yes, we are lucky, as my mom was before us. We were all born into circumstances that provided ready opportunity to education, to possibility, and to good care.

That kind of good fortune doesn't mean you're given a pass from life's challenges or its tragedies. But it does mean you get a head start. You get a privileged place in the life lane, with the least traffic and fewest obstacles. You get a better chance to contend with what life brings your way. You have access to good care when it's needed—the kind of care that offers Lynn the best chance to live for many years to come. And we have that opportunity largely because we live in a country where quality health and elder care is far too often a matter of privilege.

I think my mom would say that means it's high time to go about the business of creating a society where the care we receive isn't determined by birthplace or bank account. It's time, she'd say, to go downtown and get to work.

And so we must continue to reach out to carry others, to smile and weep with those we love. And leave, in our journey's wake, a mist that reflects the sun.

Photo by Laura Hofstadter

+

Me: It's pretty out here today, isn't it?

Adelaide: I like what's covering me.

Me: Do you mean the blanket?

Adelaide: I mean the sky.

—Adelaide Iverson, age 103

+

ACKNOWLEDGMENTS

So many people helped make this book possible ...

Lynn, I love you. Your bright spirit guides me back every time I stumble. Laura, Kevin, Hannah, and William, you fill up my life. I can't wait until the next time we jump off the dock together in Maine!

Peter, my dear late brother, who mentored so many, we will make sure your legacy endures, and to my sister-in-law Kaaren, thank you for the constancy of your love and care. Paul and Yoko, who were always with me, I love being on your team: Go Iversons! Go Stanford! Erika, Jens, Ayuko, Kate, and Ajith—my beloved nieces and nephews—you make me smile whenever I see you. Aunt Alice and my cousins Peter, Bill, Betsy, Paul, Herb, Barbara, John and Eileen—thank you for the continuing gift of family. And Ken and Gail, who knew that when our kids got married, we'd gain a fantastic friendship too?

Josh Modell, my wonderfully insightful editor, could you just explain the difference between then and than one more time? I may never get the grammar right, but you sure got the book and made it so much better. So did my writerly friends: Steve Hannah, Ron Elving, Christina

Ward, Sheila Himmel, Elizabeth Farnsworth, Ann Packer, Kate O'Donnell, Michael J. Fox, Veronique Enos, Holly Teichholz, Kathy Zonana, and Amy Yotopoulos.

Special thanks to my dedicated and tireless publishers at Light Messages—particularly Betty and Wally Turnbull and my editor Elizabeth Turnbull. And thank you Michael Croy and Northstar Literary for always believing in this book.

I have such gratitude for the understanding and encouragement my friends provided from the day I moved in with my mom through this book's completion: Dick and Judy Rubin, Gary Greenfeld and Reesa Tansey, Jim Neafsey, Margaret Cooper, James Steinbach, Ellen and Tom Hall, Kris Koenen and Joe Beyler, John Lane, Kiki Kapany and Michael Schwarz, Lynn Keller, David Leventhal, Ken Knevel and Toby Burroughs, Irene Noguchi, Greyson Bryan, Soania Mathur, Bill Wilkins, Bret Parker, Bryan Roberts, Margaret Trost and Tom Hendrickson, Jan Knecht, and Dan and Natalie Crouch.

The Menlo Park and Stanford families, friendships forged over average scotch and Adelaide's superb cooking: Kathleen and David Weisenberg, Mary Jane Parrine and Ed Ehmke, William and Susan Grindley, Lora and Mark Richardson, Dan and Peggy Hilberman, Noel and Roberta Thompson, Laurie Hofstadter and Len Shar, Doug Hofstadter, Nancy Chodorow, Joanie Chodorow, Doug Cannon, Cynthia Roberts, Louise Maier, Mary and Gerry Andeen, Fr. Xavier Lavagetto and Teresa Pleins. The spirit of 1121 Westfield Drive lives on in all of you.

Most of all, my deepest thanks go to the kind, resolute, energetic, funny, and immensely skilled women who cared for my mom, especially Sinai Latu, Eileen Khan, Roanet Morales, and Mele Taufa. You brightened my mom's life and mine—even when we were both cranky. Thanks also to Chris Brady, our wonderful hospice nurse, and to my mom's longtime physicians Margaret Forsyth and Steve Lai.

Finally, my parents Adelaide and Bill—I'll never write as well as you, Dad, but I'll keep trying to be as kind. And Mom, you're still here. You always will be.

ABOUT THE AUTHOR

DAVE IVERSON is a writer, documentary film producer, director, and retired broadcast journalist.

Dave has produced and reported more than 20 documentary specials for PBS, including the *Frontline* film, *My Father, My Brother and Me* which explored his family's battle with Parkinson's disease and

Photo by Reesa Tansey

Capturing Grace, which tells the story of what happened when a group of people with Parkinson's disease joined forces with a legendary New York City dance company.

Dave was also a radio and television reporter and host for nearly 40 years, first at Wisconsin Public Broadcasting and then at San Francisco's NPR affiliate KQED. His awards include a national Emmy, four regional Emmys, and numerous film festival citations.

Dave is a founding member of the Michael J. Fox

Foundation's Patient Council and dreams of running in one more New York City Marathon.

Winter Stars is Dave's first book. He and his wife Lynn divide their time between Oakland, California, and Boothbay Harbor, Maine. They delight in spending time with their families and grandchildren.

Follow Dave at:
www.daveiversonauthor.com